Feathers
on the
Wind

Reflections for the
Lighthearted Soul

~ Introduction ~

A Featherweight Spirituality

"Held by God...like a feather which has no weight from its own strength and lets itself be carried by the wind"—so wrote the medieval mystic, Hildegard of Bingen. Her image of a feather lightly floating on the wind is more than spiritual poetry; it gives us a way to live. Being like a feather on the wind is particularly necessary in these difficult days that teeter-totter two millennia.

Daily we are confronted with heavy issues in our personal lives: the prospect of losing a job, the specter of sickness or incurable diseases, the need to make major decisions. We are weighted down every evening in our living rooms as we look through the magical window of television and take upon ourselves the heavy burdens of social injustice, unemployment, poverty, drugs and crime—along with never-ending global conflict. Moreover, while peace should be the fruit of prayer and religion, even these can at times make our hearts heavy with the problems of sin and guilt, with moral obligations, with all the difficulties in praying.

Held earthbound not only by earth's gravitational field but by all these other forces of gravity, we need to imitate Hildegard and strive to live as lightly as a feather borne by the Breath of God. That Divine Wind, the Spirit, was promised to us—and God keeps every promise. We need only to let go, to float on the mystery of God's abiding love and care for us.

The brief featherweight reflections in this book are intended for busy people looking for a lift. Long ago it was believed that the *feathers* of birds enabled them to defy gravity and fly. There are legends about the first aviators who made garments out of feathers to lift themselves up into flight. Hildegard, however, reminds us that "the feather flew, not because of anything in itself but because the air bore it along." In themselves these reflections have no power to give you the gift of flight, but they encourage the kind of trust that Hildegard possessed, the feather-like quality that lifts your heart and soul to God.

Featherweight is a term used for extreme lightness. It refers, for example, to the lightest weight that a racehorse can carry in a handicap or to the very lightest boxer. In the paper trade, the name is given to very light, antique, loosely woven book papers. For theologians and serious spiritual writers, the loosely woven reflections of this book are without doubt "featherweight," but they can help in the very *weighty* task of cultivating a true lightness of being. These brief meditations court humor and a light-hearted insight that will ground you in the wisdom of the Spirit while helping you to float on the Wind of God.

There was once a king sitting on his throne....It pleased the king to raise a small feather from the ground and he commanded it to fly. The feather flew, not because of anything in itself but because the air bore it along. Thus I am a... Feather on the Breath of God.

– Hildegard of Bingen

~ Chapter 1 ~

Nine Feathers on
Flexibility and Rigidity

How to Avoid Distress
Over Life's Problems

Life is full of problems that weigh us down, and we all have our share of them. If we want to live like a feather on the Wind—if we want to be lighthearted—we need to examine our major problems and how we respond to them.

One of our chief contemporary concerns is how we appear to others. On an average day we Americans spend about $50,000,000 on beauty goods and services! Each day some 1,600 of us have plastic surgery to improve our looks, 200 have face-lifts, and 225 receive newly shaped noses. And since slim is in, every day over 100,000,000 Americans are dieting.

A heightened consciousness about good health can cause legitimate concern about our weight. If we dieters are honest, however, most of us have to admit that our major motivation lies in improving our appearance. When that kind of concern becomes a preoccupation, it can literally take over our life-energy. That's especially true with issues of food, which can have a dramatic effect on our lives.

Imagine, for example, how your life would change if your primary concern were feeding yourself. You might be perpetually caught up in finding new ways to satisfy your hunger. Your favorite reading material would be cookbooks, especially illustrated ones. You would spend a lot of time in the kitchen or visiting grocery stores. Your preoccupation might even lead you to change your profession; you might become a cook or waiter so that you could be constantly surrounded with food.

Interestingly, Jesus advises us to cultivate such a preoccupation with diet. He tells us to be a hungry people: "Blessed are those who hunger and thirst for

holiness" (Mt. 5: 6). Yet paradoxically, if holiness is our core concern, we don't become overly concerned over life's minor issues, which we usually inflate out of proportion. Those whose primary problem is the hunger to be holy, the ravishing appetite to be godlike, have the ability to see the real size of life's problems. Because they are borne through life by the Spirit of God, they remain light as a feather even when their problems seem heavy.

A simple exercise might help in keeping that lighthearted perspective. When a flat tire makes you late for an appointment, instead of becoming angry you can pray this mini-prayer: "So what! What does being late have to do with my real concern today?" Even in its simple form, that midget prayer "So what!" is a powerful deflator of those problems that cause our blood pressure to soar and our heads to ache.

The next time your computer goes down, a birthday party flops or an August rainstorm ruins your picnic, just chant your "So what!" prayer. Pause for a second and place the moment's disaster within the framework of your life's greatest concern: being godlike. You may find that what first appeared as a disaster is really a gift-opportunity to increase your holy hunger, an opportunity to reinforce your reliance on the Holy Wind.

Besides, if your new mini-prayer "So what!" can become a habit, you may find that you are not among the over 200,000 Americans who on an average day visit a doctor, complaining of a headache!

Need to Make a Decision?

A rabbi renowned for his holiness tried to teach his followers to seek answers within themselves rather than merely relying on him for advice. His disciples, however, continued lining up outside his office to ask his opinion on various moral issues and to seek his counsel. Finally, the rabbi placed a sign on his door: "Any Two Questions Answered for $100."

The long line outside his office disappeared. One of his wealthiest followers, however, after some deliberation, brought him two important questions. Handing over his money, the man asked, "Isn't $100 rather costly for just two questions?" "Yes it is," said the rabbi, "and your second question?"

This isn't just a Jewish joke; it's a parable about the tradition of seeking answers from spiritual leaders. The Gospels report that such questions frequently were asked of Jesus. In America in the 1890s, our immigrant ancestors, who had little formal education, expected their parish priest to have answers to a wide variety of concerns, from what was or wasn't a mortal sin to which candidate to vote for.

Old habits are hard to break, and going to "experts" for answers to our moral questions is one of them. To seek advice in legal, business and religious matters only makes good sense. However, if pastors and spiritual directors charged per question (like the rabbi in the story—and like lawyers today), those with pockets full of moral questions might spend more time in prayer!

One way to answer a moral question is to reach for the telephone and call "Father." Those answers can also be found by prayerful reflection on the Word of God in Holy Scripture and by patient sitting-with a question in prayer. The Second Vatican Council challenged us to take more responsibility for forming

our own consciences. It also underlined the principle of freedom of conscience—the fact that experts can't compel us to accept a particular answer—when it taught: "In religious matters no one is to be forced to act in a manner contrary to his or her beliefs" (*Declaration on Religious Freedom*).

Taking responsibility for one's personal moral decisions can be painful, but pain is part of any emotional and spiritual growth. It can be disturbing when our heart tells us one thing and our head another. It is unsettling when, instead of a powerful authoritarian voice, the only certitude we have is in a small, quiet inner voice. Good decisions are made by listening to both head and heart, to the voice of authority and the inner voice. This way of addressing our questions, however, takes time and patience.

The good news is that Jesus promised that those who loved him would have roomers! "If you love me, the Father and I will take up our dwelling within you" (see Jn. 14: 23). Whenever we are faced with a moral choice or an important decision, we should recall his words, "Knock and it will be opened, ask and you shall receive" (see Mt. 7: 7). Knock on the door of those Sacred Roomers who dwell in your heart and ask them for advice. When we fail to seek the guidance of the Divine Wisdom within us, we quickly lose the ability to find our own answers to our spiritual questions, and we never access a whole range of God-given resources.

Learn a lesson from the unique situation of the birds of New Zealand. That island nation probably has more flightless birds, like the kiwi and the penguin, than any other country on earth. Scientists say that long ago these birds could fly, but because they had an endless supply of food and no natural predators, they had no reason to exercise that God-given ability. Eventually their great gift was lost!

How to Not Suffer
From Liberation Cramps

"Don't swim for an hour after you eat" was a law we all embraced as if it had been given by God to Moses on Mt. Sinai. For the past fifty years at home and at school this commandment of a Red Cross water-safety pamphlet has been religiously followed. It stated that swimming immediately after eating would produce cramps, possibly causing a swimmer to drown. According to Alfie Kohn's book, *The Truth About Popular Beliefs*, however, that cardinal rule is really a misconception! Not a single documented case has ever been reported of someone drowning as a result of swimming on a full stomach. While it's only wise not to engage in any strenuous activity after a large meal, going for a swim after eating is not a death sentence.

When I learned about the fallacy of that Red Cross guideline, I had twin reactions. First, I smiled to myself as I reflected that yet another solemn belief had been unmasked. At the same time, I felt mildly disturbed because of all the enjoyment I had lost as a kid waiting that "holy hour" after lunch before I could go swimming. My second reaction is not an uncommon one (and is often more than a mild disturbance) when religious laws are removed—even when they are recognized as misconceptions. So many of us are not free enough to walk out of the prison of law, whether that law is taught by the Red Cross or Religion.

Those who wish to live like a feather on the Wind should take a look at the degree of their personal freedom. Take a few moments for an inventory of the conceptions and beliefs you would be willing to abandon if they were shown to be misconceptions. For example, it was once commonly accepted that a major power would become weak if it had a woman

leader—that is, until Golda Meir, Indira Gandhi and Maggie Thatcher made their marks. Fifty years ago people also believed that a Catholic could never be president or that African-Americans were inferior to White Americans. Often bias and prejudice are the illegitimate parents of those beliefs that can steal our freedom and rob us as a society.

What is the measure of your ability to embrace the radical freedom of Christ's love? Take a few minutes to parade prayerfully before your mind such liberating concepts as a Moslem, Jewish or gay President, a woman as a Catholic bishop or a time when non-violent peacemakers are greeted with ticker-tape parades. Then examine your reactions as these concepts, and any others your imagination can call forth, parade past. Do any of them cause you cramps? If so, the reason probably isn't because you prayed this Parade Prayer immediately after dinner, but rather because you aren't as free as you thought. If you suffer from the distress of concept cramps when old beliefs are abandoned, here is a prayer for divine relief:

O God, you led your children out of slavery in Egypt
   and sent your Son Jesus
   to liberate us from sin and selfishness.
O Merciful God, whose middle name is Freedom,
   help me to be free of the pain
      caused by new concepts
   that liberate me as they allow others to be
   all that you created them to be.
May that renewed freedom
   allow me to live in a lighthearted love,
   borne by the breath of your Holy Spirit.
I ask this in the name of the great liberator, Jesus.
Amen.

How to Weasel Your Way into Heaven

St. Jordan of Battberg had a pet weasel as a regular companion. In pictures of the saint, his pet weasel is always at his side. That in itself may be enough to suggest the weasel as a model for those who seek holiness. The weasel is a graceful and intelligent animal. While the smallest of carnivores, the weasel is said to be superior in combat to animals much larger than itself. Its determination and resourcefulness should confirm its status as a good image for a modern disciple of Christ!

Nevertheless, the weasel might still seem a strange choice as a paradigm for discipleship. This clever creature has long had a negative image as being sneaky or cowardly. The weasel's bad reputation comes largely from its style of parental care. It slyly moves from place to place to protect its young from harm, exhibiting a singular ability to slip in and out of tight places.

Medieval legend also has it that the weasel would rather be killed than tread on muddy ground. This reputation grew out of a belief that weasels only visit clear streams and grassy woodlands. Yet even when we see how some of the weasel's "bad press" is based on misconceptions, it may be hard to believe that in the Middle Ages the weasel ranked with the lily and dove among the living symbols of the innocence of Christ.

In any case, this may be the ideal time for the revival of the weasel as a Christian symbol. With its long, fluid body, the form of the weasel speaks of great flexibility. Jesus praised that virtue as extremely important for his disciples if they were to be faithful to the fresh spirit of the Gospels. The new wine of

Jesus was—and is—too powerful for old wine skins; it needs a flexible container.

The true disciple is the one who is flexible to the point of elasticity, especially in this age of great change. Like a weasel, we need to be able and eager to bend and give if we are to adapt the Good News to the constantly changing patterns of our society and the world. Yet, in spite of Jesus' words about the need for supple carriers of his message, that charism of flexibility is rarely listed among the desired virtues of the Holy Spirit.

The rapid changes in the world over the past few years have required enormous flexibility in politics and business. Changes just as radical are also taking place in our personal and religious lives. Yet often they are met with rigid, outdated laws and ideas. In religion and in every aspect of our lives, we must be able to adapt. Encouraged by the inspirational images of both the dove and the weasel, we need to storm heaven for that greatly needed gift of God's Spirit: elasticity.

When next you're faced with a situation in which both you and your problem refuse to give an inch, recall St. Jordan's pet weasel. Be as resourceful as a weasel protecting its young. Also be willing to give a little, to be flexible, without judging yourself as spineless or lacking in principles. If you are true to the Spirit, there is great strength in flexibility. Pray to the Spirit for the gift of a flexible heart so that, like the powerful weasel, you'll be pliable enough to do whatever you are asked to do by God—so that you can "weasel" your way into heaven!

Elephant Pegs

One of the great treats for me as a small boy growing up in the Midwest was the day the Ringling Brothers Circus came to town. In those depression years, the circus still performed under the big top rather than in an auditorium. It was high adventure when the circus train pulled onto a siding near the flour mill elevators to unload its animals, tents and wonders from the seven seas. Almost as exciting as the circus itself was watching the workers set up the big top and the surrounding tent city of the sideshows. This tent raising required the combined effort of men and elephants.

The elephants in the circus did double duty. They were prized performers in the circus acts as well as beasts of burden for raising the tents. I recall seeing them chained to large wooden pegs driven into the ground before their entrance into the big top. I've often wondered how animals so powerful could be contained by a simple peg in the ground. Why didn't those huge elephants simply pull up the wooden peg and walk away?

Recently I learned the answer to that elephant question. It seems that a baby elephant is trained by being chained to a concrete post buried deep in the earth. Should a young elephant tug at the post with all its might, it would be unable to pull it out of the earth. The result of such childhood training is that later in life it will never attempt to pull up the post to which it is chained, even one that easily could be yanked out of the ground!

If we wish to soar featherlike on the Wind, then we need to be free of anything that chains us earthbound, especially any elephantine childhood restraints. Each of us has been restricted by childhood statements and attitudes both at home and at school

which still shackle us today. While we have outgrown many of our childhood weaknesses, we are still often easily chained by the words of Mom or Dad, a teacher or friend. Like those strong adult circus elephants, we can remain tied down by echoes of "You're no good" or "Dear, you can't do that."

Whatever keeps us staked to a post with the words "You can't" written on it restricts the exercise of the gifts given us by God. All such restraints are handicaps to our spirituality. So, today, take an inventory of all the things you believe you can't do. List each of them on a piece of paper and study them carefully. Weed out the ones you don't need or that won't help you become holy. Then, write in bold red crayon across the top of your paper, "With God, all things are possible!"

Pickpockets of the Heart

On an average day 11,800 American homes are burglarized. Each of us hopes that ours will not be one of them! The act of a thief is a double crime: Not only are we robbed of our possessions, we are violated by our personal living space being entered and probed without permission. Depending on where you live, the odds are that your home will be robbed at least once in your lifetime. Since robbery is so much a part of contemporary life, it needs to be dealt with in our spirituality. What attitude of the heart should we take toward those who break into our homes or steal our purse?

Perhaps the most common initial attitude that we experience is shock, followed by anger or outrage. Consider, however, the attitude that appears in the book of Proverbs: "Despise not the thief if he steals to satisfy his appetite when he is hungry" (Prv. 6: 30).

Still, since the earliest times stealing has been a consciously chosen profession more often than the last resort of a poor person. Because of that, it's easy to judge all thieves to be professional crooks who are too lazy to work or out to get big rewards without earning them. With the widespread abuse of drugs, it's also easy to presume that thieves are drug addicts in need of money to support their habit. But as disciples of Jesus, are we not to abstain from such judgment?

The next line in that quotation from Proverbs sums up our contemporary sense of criminal justice, even if the person who robs us is in dire need. Verse 31 says, "Yet, if he be caught he must pay back sevenfold; all the wealth of his house he may yield up." Jesus challenges us to move beyond the law. We are called not only to refrain from despising the thief, but to love him or her. Loving one's enemies is easy

as long as it is a generic idea. It's easy if the one to be loved and blessed hasn't caused us any personal harm or loss.

Remember the classic television commercial that urged us to keep from falling victim to thieves and pickpockets by "not leaving home without it." As disciples of Christ, that "it" doesn't mean traveler's checks or a credit card. Never leave home, whether to go to the store or on vacation, without having Jesus' attitude of love and non-judgment. Even though our chances of being victims of robbery in one form or another are very great, a Christlike attitude prevents us from really being robbed. The worst thievery is when our peace and love are stolen from us and all that's left are anger and hate. When that happens, we are *really* twice robbed.

Don't wait until you're mugged to try to practice this special brand of love. Practice it before you're robbed, cheated or the victim of some injustice. There are many opportunities for such practice: someone cutting in front of you during morning traffic or stealing a choice parking space, a person reaching over you to take the last "anything," or a "thief" who steals your good name by words of slander. While this practice isn't easy and the rewards aren't always obvious, they are deep: "Blessed is the householder whom the thief does not find asleep" (see Lk. 12: 37-39).

Try the Third Way

Part of the genius of Jesus was shown in his unusual solutions to life's problems. When asked how to respond to an insult, for example, he offered a unique strategy. There were two traditional ways to answer an insult: pretending not to hear the insult or flinging back an insult—or a fist—in return. Jesus invited us to try a third way: returning a blessing for the insult. This invitation to a peaceful solution is not just Palestinian poetry; it's a guideline for living as a peacemaker.

Such invitations of Jesus were radical and inventive solutions to the problems of his day. They remain, even today, as fresh and creative as ever. Whatever the problem you may face, consider an alternative solution, the Third Way, the Way of Jesus. May the following parable serve as a battery jumper for your personal creativity. The problem at the heart of the parable is a flesh and blood one, a conflict taken from real life.

Once upon a time there was a commuter who each morning walked from the train station to her office along the same street. Every day she would encounter the very same beggar at the same busy intersection. This beggar, instead of calling out for money from those who passed by, had a unique approach to the ancient art of begging.

Not only was he in a wheelchair, but each day, just as the crowd of morning commuters came down the street, he would be carefully positioned in the gutter, struggling to get his wheelchair up over the curb. As if on cue, the commuter would spring to help the beggar get his wheelchair up on the sidewalk. Without even pausing to say "thank you," he would whisper in her ear, "For the love of Christ, lady, can you spare a dollar for a poor cripple?" Whether or

not she gave him anything, she would always boil over in rage. She would storm into work full of anger at being suckered by the clever beggar.

Her friends at work would ask, "Why do you stop to help him? It's an obvious trap. Just let him struggle!" While the advice made sense, she couldn't take it. She found it impossible not to stop and offer some assistance to the crippled beggar, even if it was only a ruse. For weeks she prayed over the problem. It seemed she had only two choices: to continue to be a sucker, with the backlash of anger at being taken advantage of, or to risk becoming insensitive to others in need. Then one day she jumped to her feet and danced around her living room, delighted that she had found the perfect solution.

The next morning on her way to work, she rushed to the Western Auto store, then eagerly went on to the corner where, as usual, the beggar was struggling to get his wheelchair up on the sidewalk. "Ah, having trouble as usual with your wheelchair? I have a gift for you," she said, handing him a large paper sack. Then she walked away down the street, singing to herself. The beggar opened the bag. Inside were two plastic wheel ramps!

The Secret of Fuller, the Brush Man

Today they usually visit your home by telephone, but not too long ago they rang your doorbell. The most famous of all those door-to-door salesmen—who became the subject of endless jokes—was the Fuller Brush Man. Alfred Carl Fuller, however, was certainly no joke! His is the classic American success story. He arrived in America from Nova Scotia in 1905 with only seventy-five dollars, a Bible and a habit of daydreaming. He was fired from one job after another for being irresponsible or incompetent and finally decided that he was tired of working for other people. In 1905 he began his own business of selling brushes from door to door.

By night he labored with his wire and bristles, designing new kinds of brushes for the early twentieth century home. To Alfred's surprise he discovered that he was a gifted salesman. His small company was so successful that by 1910 he employed twenty-five other men to sell his array of brushes. Fuller was a religious man who married a biblical devotion to a mule-like stubbornness. He refused to let the memory of past failures and firings hold him back.

In 1919 his young company faced a serious threat with the invention of the vacuum cleaner, which was advertised as "the end to the drudgery of sweeping." Fuller struck back with ads that advised women to take up sweeping as a means to offset ills, as "an exercise of a highly beneficial nature." As the vacuum sweeper grew in popularity, Fuller expanded his company's merchandise to include all types of cleaning products. When he retired in 1943, the once nearly penniless Fuller was president of a company with sales that topped ten million dollars a year! Alfred

Fuller is a true-life parable.

We can learn a moral from Fuller's refusal to lay down as a failure after being fired again and again—and from his belief in his daydreams. His hope-filled belief in himself and in his dreams was written large in his Bible, the single possession with which he entered this country: "True faith is contagious. It spreads from God to oneself and one's abilities. Faith makes us see differently what the world judges as failures—like the cross of Christ. Faith is living with hope in the truth that God desires good things for each of us, if only we are willing to take risks and trust."

Fuller took numerous risks in his life. At the same time, he was resilient and flexible enough to adjust to the "sweeping" changes in his chosen field. He also chose to be deaf to the echoes of past failures and firings, to the charge that he was inept. As we strive to become all that God desires us to be, we must learn how to handle our past mistakes. Like toxic wastes, they often easily poison us and kill our hopes and dreams. At best they weigh us down, preventing us from being lighthearted. A wholesome spirituality always includes answering the doorbell with a smile when a new dream, like a traveling salesman, comes peddling itself at our door.

Boo!

President Calvin Coolidge was known to hide in the bushes around the White House and jump out to scare his Secret Service bodyguards! Imagine this presidential playtime in reverse, with Secret Service agents hiding in closets and jumping out to scare the president! Yet that kind of twist of humor is not uncommon today. In our crime-conscious society, people often attempt to protect their property and themselves with heavy locks, bars on the windows and elaborate security systems. They are ever alert and defensive in public for thieves or those who might do them harm.

While prudent, this attitude can also be self-defeating. For consider how your various systems for protecting yourself, your property and all your possessions can actually scare you by creating not a climate of security but rather of anxiety and mistrust.

If you live in such fear, try playing the Calvin Coolidge game on your secret service agents. You might, for example, sneak up on your double-locked and barred door and shout, "BOO!"

~ Chapter 2 ~

Nine Feathers on
Change and
New Beginnings

Columbus' Spice for a Dull Life

As we have seen, living like a feather on the Wind requires a certain flexibility. Such lightheartedness also calls for a willingness to change, to embark on new beginnings. When we think of famous new beginnings, perhaps the first one that comes to mind is the venture begun by Christopher Columbus.

Think of his crew's sense of anticipation—and their fears—as they set out on their great voyage. And what fueled the dreams of Columbus and his crew? It was spices! Every schoolchild knows that the discovery of the Americas was an accident, that their destination was India, the fabled Cathay, and their desired bounty was spices. As good as gold were pepper, ginger and cinnamon, since a single shipload of spices could make one rich for life! Furthermore, the nation that controlled the spice trade to a great extent controlled the commerce of Europe. Before refrigeration, spices were needed to preserve food, disguise poor-tasting dishes and salvage sour wine. Spices were also employed in embalming and in making incense, perfume and medicine. The rare spices of the Orient "spiced up" dull food and *life*.

Like fifteenth century Europeans, we seem to be in need of exotic spices from far distant lands to enliven our dull lives. Is that not a possible answer to why the richest country in the world has the greatest need for illegal—and legal—drugs? What kind of new spice could counter that need? As in the days of Columbus, what spice could make you rich for life if you sailed into port with a shipload of it?

Unlike salt which isn't healthy for those with heart problems, there is a new spice that has no negative side effects. It would not be a surprise if the *New England Journal of Medicine* announced in its next issue that this new spice actually improves health and

vitalizes the entire nervous system. As with pepper, cinnamon and nutmeg, at first only the wealthy will be able to afford this new, rare spice which will make any dull, bland food, drink or activity suddenly dance with delight. After years of being *the* spice of the privileged few, however, it will take its place, along with the salt and pepper, on everyone's table.

It will be so powerful a spice that people will keep it on their bedside table and carry it to work or wherever they go in a handy pocket-container. Since table spice shakers are usually of the same shape and design, for identification they are marked with the first letter of the spice's name, like "S" or "P." The shaker of the new spice which will complete the tabletop trinity of spices will bear the large letter "G."

Sprinkle this spice on anything that you find dull or bland, sour or tainted, lifeless or ordinary, and I promise you it will instantly come alive with taste and pleasure. Sprinkle it on your daily work, and you will experience a rare joy in your labor. Daily sprinkle some of it on those you love and live with, and you will see them with new eyes. Sprinkle it generously on your problems and difficulties, and even they will be radically transformed.

The good news is that unlike the rare spices of the fifteenth century, you don't need a shipload of it. Those who possess even small amounts of it can be rich for life. And, the really *good* news is that you don't have to sail around the world to India or take a camel caravan to Tibet to obtain life's most important spice: *Gratitude!*

Cowards Never Started

Columbus' journal entry for October 8, 1492, reads, "Thanks be to God, the breezes were softer than in April at Seville...they are so laden with scent...the men could now bear no more; they complained of the long voyage." When we struggle to break through to our own new world, we should remember the frustration and fear of Columbus' crew. That October 9th, not knowing that he was only days away from sighting land, Columbus told his crew that if land wasn't reached in two or three days, "...(you may) cut off my head and you shall return!"

Like Columbus' comrades, we also can live in frustration, with a sense of lost dreams. We also can become impatient and depressed when success delays her arrival. While we often contrast the courage of Columbus with the lack of belief and the fear of his crew, they also need our praise and applause. Was it not truly heroic of them even to have begun such a journey? It obviously would have been much safer for them to remain at home.

In the Iowa capitol building is a mural of pioneers crossing the prairies. Underneath it is the inscription, "The coward never started, the weak fell by the way." Those words apply not only to the crews of those three small ships which left Spain for the Indies, but to anyone who has the courage to set forth on the journey of the Way of Christ. Cowards never even attempt it—or anything new or difficult—and the weak jump ship before they are out of port.

Reflecting on the great venture of Columbus can inspire each of us to take risks, to leave home on a voyage of discovery. The French writer, Marcel Proust, invites us to a Columbus-like voyage when he writes, "The only real voyage of discovery consists not in seeking new landscapes but in having new eyes." Jesus

echoes that challenge with his words, "Have you eyes but no sight?" (See Mk. 8:15). That invitation to a new kind of vision has the power to transform the ordinary into the extraordinary, a simple trip to the store into a voyage of incredible discovery.

Cataracts caused by the commonplace can blind us, causing us to dream of the beauty of far-off lands, the excitement of places other than where we are. It is said that everyone is living out someone else's fantasy! Part of a spirit-voyage of discovery is to see yourself, your home, work and daily life through another's eyes. Look at what's ordinary in your life through the eyes of someone living in the third world, a slum resident in some inner city or even the person who lives next door! See your life with new eyes, enjoy it and wildly give thanks.

We can commemorate the new world adventure of Columbus and his crew with a devout prayer for the gift of new eyes. We can put flesh and bone on those prayers by scrubbing our old eyes clean of the cataracts of the commonplace. Look at anything, slowly blink three times as you make a visual sign of the cross and then look again. With ever-new eyes, you can make your daily drive to work, a trip to the store, even a walk around the neighborhood into a voyage as rich and exciting as the epic journey of Columbus. Such an adventure is at your fingertips. It is also an essential part of the voyage-way of Jesus, the way of giving thanks always and for everything.

An Ageless Fresh Start

We all desire to make changes in our lives: to lose weight, stop smoking, alter some troublesome inter-personal patterns or overcome some handicap. Our most common mistake in making our resolutions stick is probably using the word "should" instead of "must"! Studies, however, have shown that even when people are determined to alter their lives, they usually fail to make lasting changes. The additional ingredient we need to turn the impossible into the possible is finding a role model!

While it's common to think that role models are only useful for the young, we need them at each stage of our lives. Do not all of us have some affliction, physical or otherwise, that limits what we can do and therefore who we are? One role model that we all—whether white-haired seniors or teenagers—could use in overcoming our limitations is that senior-senior citizen, Grandma Moses!

As a youth Anna Mary Robertson worked on a farm where she met and married a hired hand, Tom Moses. They moved to their own farm and raised ten children. Anna loved needlework, but as she grew older her hands were stiffened by arthritis. At age eighty she could no longer handle a needle and decided to try her hand at painting! She painted farm scenes from memory and gave a few to the local drugstore.

One day a New York City art collector passing through town saw her simple, childlike paintings. The rest, as they say, is history—art history. For Grandma Moses became one of America's classic folk-painters, gaining an international following. While she didn't start painting until age eighty, she finished over 1,500 paintings, one-fourth of them after she was over 100 years old! Aged, worn down by a hard life, without

any art training and crippled by arthritis, Anna Moses still gifted the world with great beauty and wonder.

Regardless of our age, Anna Moses is a true role model for how God's grace can overcome any defeat, drawback or deficiency for those who are willing to risk doing the impossible. The mystery of the cross of Christ shouts out this lesson about how, with God's help, we can turn any adversity into an advantage.

Besides seeds of determination and the presence of a good role model, one further ingredient we need to make lasting changes is the courage to risk making failures. As Anthony Robbins has said, "There are no failures—only outcomes!" Robbins maintains that success is the result of good judgment, which is the result of experience. Experience, however, is often gained at the expense of bad judgment and mistakes. So as you strive to turn your life around for the better, do not fear making mistakes. They are only seeds— for anyone clever enough to learn from them. From the seeds of our mistakes grow the fruits of wisdom and good judgment, which in turn produce the harvest of success, a la Grandma Moses.

Words to Live and Die By

"I do not know which is the more difficult in a Christian life, to live well or die well." These were the last words spoken by Daniel Defoe, author of *Robinson Crusoe*. As a writer, I wonder what words I will choose to say just before death kisses my lips. Because death is one of life's great new beginnings and because I desire to live as light as a feather, I decided to take on that choice as a spiritual exercise.

Almost daily, devastating natural disasters, global wars and violent crime reminds us that death waits around the next corner—for each of us. What shall we say when we turn that corner? William Porter, whose pen name was O'Henry, turned the corner and said, "Turn up the lights; I don't want to go home in the dark." I like that bit about "going home," since that's the way I view death. "Let me go, let me go," were the last words of Clara Barton, founder of the American Red Cross. Her words would be especially appropriate if I were dying wired up to a battery of medical machines: "Let me go!"

If I wanted to make a statement with my dying words, I would copy those of Edward "Death Valley Scotty" Scott. He was an American recluse whose last words were, "I got four things to live by: don't say nothin' that will hurt anyone; don't give advice— nobody will take it anyway; don't complain; don't explain." It's hard to beat that for a personal creed, but it's a bit long—if you're dying.

As I pondered my death-moment spiritual exercise, I turned to the Bible. What better words to have on one's lips as one dies than those used by Jesus. It seems, however, that there's some confusion about what they were. John reported them as, "Now it is finished" (Jn.19: 30). Matthew and Mark recorded Jesus as saying, "My God, my God, why have you

forsaken me?" (Mt. 27: 46; Mk. 15: 34). In Luke, Jesus said, "Father, into your hands I commend my spirit" (Lk. 23: 46). Choosing among them, I prefer Luke's version.

Having read this far, perhaps you're beginning to feel a bit like Karl Marx. His last words were to his housekeeper. She had asked him if he had a final message for the world. Marx's curt reply was, "Go on, get out! Last words are for fools who haven't said enough." The fact that Marx was angry at the request for a dying statement is understandable. Personally, though, I wouldn't want to die with angry words on my lips. I'd prefer to go with a dash of fun as did James W. Rogers. Convicted of murder and executed in 1960 in Utah, Rogers was able to keep a sense of humor, even in the face of a firing squad. When asked if he had a final request, Rogers' last words were, "Why, yes—a bulletproof vest."

While each of these famous last words have a certain value, my final choice has to be those of the Congregationalist preacher, Henry Ward Beecher. His dying words in 1887 were, "Now comes the mystery." They are my choice for several reasons. I've always distrusted those who have had death and the next life all explained and defined. I also like Beecher's words since my favorite name for God is "The Divine Mystery." Finally, I like them because I agree with the Orthodox Archimandrite Barnabas who said, "Protestants say there is no mystery, Roman Catholics explain all mysteries, Orthodoxy says all is Mystery."

I hope this meditation will inspire you to take up a pencil and paper and reflect upon what you would say at that historic moment of your life. Whether you actually use those words or not, I assure you that this exercise can be most valuable. It will, in a play on the dying words of Daniel Defoe, help you not only to die well but also *live* well.

How to Avoid Dying

A recent *Farmer's Almanac* contained a list of things to avoid if you don't want to die! Among them are these interesting bits of advice: "Keep cats off the piano keys....Never place a broom on a bed....Don't rock an empty rocking chair....Don't sing in bed....Don't walk around in only one shoe....Don't count the cars in a funeral procession....Be sure that someone else cooks your birthday dinner." I would like to add one more way to keep from dying: "Don't take up the Way of Christ!"

For Jesus tells us clearly: "If you wish to be my disciple, you must deny your very self, take up your cross and begin to follow in my footsteps....Those who lose their lives for my sake will find them" (Mt. 16: 24-25).

As anyone who has tried knows, such dying to self is not at all easy to do. The history of spirituality is crowded with traditionally accepted ways to die to self, including fasting, self-denial and harsh disciplines. Unfortunately, all disciplines emphasize willpower and self-mastery. As a result, unless they are truly grounded in humility, ascetical practices whose purpose is denial of self tend to add more power to the ego-self, which takes pride in accomplishing difficult denial disciplines.

Jesus spoke directly to this problem when he urged care in embracing the classic self-denying disciplines of fasting, prayer and the giving of alms. In short he said, "Be on your guard. Beware of doing things of which you can be proud." He cautioned that fasting, alms-giving and prayer be done secretly (See Mt. 6: 1-17).

Jesus went even further in proposing denial of self to his disciples. He encouraged his followers to forget themselves by placing others first. Instead of

harsh disciplines, we are called to invest ourselves in acts of humble service to family, friends and stranger.

The most effective acts of self-denial are those performed as part of the secret service! I am not referring to the government's Secret Service, to those who have the duty of protecting the president from assassination. Yet a sacred secret service will guard you from self-aggrandizement and protect your spirit.

Secret service involves performing little acts of unrequested service to others with whom you live or work. The most rewarding disciplines would be those deeds performed without others even knowing who it was who had helped them. Such secret service could be cleaning the cat's litter box—even when it's not your cat! It could be picking up after others, emptying a wastebasket or shining a pair of shoes. You could choose to do for others those chores they dislike doing, even if you don't find them enjoyable either.

"Don't sing in bed" was one of the counsels of the old *Farmer's Almanac* if you didn't want to die. If you really don't want to die, remember whenever you give to a charity to make your donation public! Demand that they put up a brass plaque with your name on it! If don't want to die, make your prayers long and praise God loudly in public places. If you don't want to die, "don't rock an empty rocking chair," and also fast and abstain often—especially during Lent—and make a big deal about it! Brag about your fasting, complain about having to eat tuna, and look down your nose at those who don't abstain.

Regardless of what you avoid—if you want to avoid dying—whatever you do, don't engage in secret service!

Rest and Live in Peace

Our most popular prayer for the dead is "May they rest in peace." Since our lives are so busy, it's no wonder we would wish our loved ones rest. In the days when Latin was the universal language of the Church, the funeral Mass was called a rest Mass or *Requiem.* That title came from the opening words of the Gregorian Chant that began every Mass for the dead: *Requiem eternam dona eis, Domine*, "Eternal rest grant to them, O Lord."

Since life here is so hectic, we pray that the dead might find eternal rest in paradise. But was Jesus simply talking about burial insurance when he said, "Come to me all you who find life a burden, and I will give your souls rest" (Mt. 11: 28)? Was he not offering rest for us today, rest from the burdens and busy pace of our lives?

Once upon a time there was a woman who longed to find out what heaven is like. She prayed constantly, "O God, grant me in this life a vision of paradise." She prayed in this way for years until one night she had a dream. In her dream an angel came and led her to heaven. They walked down a street in paradise until they came to an ordinary looking house. The angel, pointing toward the house, said, "Go and look inside."

So the woman walked in the house and found a person preparing supper, another reading the newspaper, and children playing with their toys. Naturally, she was disappointed and returned to the angel on the street. "Is this all there is to heaven?"

The angel replied, "Those people you saw in that house are not in paradise, paradise is in them!"

At this very moment, even as you read this, paradise is in you—if you are in Christ. The endless restlessness of our lives is the result of forgetting that

fact. Eternal peace is indeed a gift awaiting us, but peace can be a *present reality* that only reaches its maturity beyond the grave. Besides, if you fail to find peace here, how will you find it beyond the grave?

We often see this life as a burden, weighted down with cares and struggles and, therefore, devoid of peacefulness. That worldview, however, is really due less to God's design than to how we respond to life's problems. Because we think of peace as an absence of difficulties, we usually want something or someone out there to change so that our problems will go away. But our problems are no more than homework, the homework of holiness that calls for us to change. When we do the daily work of transforming our way of thinking and responding into the Way of Christ, then no "problem" can disturb our peace.

Finally, if we want to live like a feather on the Wind, we need to add another assignment to our homework of transformation. We should strive at least once a day to taste the peace of paradise that dwells within us. We need to find some time each day to sit quietly in peace, in stillness, savoring the mystery of God within us. Such silent sitting will not only prepare us to find "eternal rest" at the time of our death, it will help us find infinite peace in the midst of the problems of life.

A Titanic Hymn
For the Autumn of Life

On the night of April 14, 1912, the White Star Liner Titanic, on her maiden voyage across the Atlantic, sank after striking an iceberg at full speed. The giant ocean liner, considered by experts to be "unsinkable," had lifeboats for only half of its 2,200 passengers, and so almost 1,500 lost their lives. As women and children filled the small boats and the male passengers lined the decks, the ship's band played ragtime jazz. As the fortunate-but-heavy-hearted survivors sailed off from the Titanic, they could hear the lively music and see the portholes ablaze with lights as the ship slowly sank. At 2:20 A.M. on April 15, when the water began flowing over the deck, the bandmaster, Mr. Hartley, tapped his violin to signal the other musicians to cease playing ragtime. As the ocean liner tilted and started to slip under the waves, the band began to play the old Episcopal hymn "Autumn."

If you listen carefully on an October night, you can hear echoes of that old hymn in the evening air. Each time the season of autumn blazes out with golden beauty, another year is sinking in the ocean of time. Yet autumn is not just a season of the year; it has a timeless quality. It speaks of a season of our lives, of our times of transition, of the passing of institutions and eras.

When we listen to the sounds of autumn's hymn, it's filled with tales about that cold night in April of 1912. There are stories of the passengers who remained on the ship's deck in formal evening attire so that they could die with dignity. Stories of the last hours of the Titanic abound with deeds of heroism, acts of unselfishness and love-filled departures between husbands and wives who knew they would

never see each other again. The nearness of death has the power to call forth a keen awareness of what is truly important in life.

Blessed are those for whom autumn's golden hymn of death is a reveille. Blessed are those who are awakened to how short is the time left in their lives for acts of generosity, heroism and affection. Blessed are those for whom the lessening of hours of light and the smell of burning leaves is a reminder to value more keenly the gifts of their lives. Blessed are those for whom the chill of a fall night and the melody of autumn's winds is an aid to see their problems and pains in their correct proportion. Blessed are they, for they shall enjoy life immensely.

Blessed are those who can live as if they were aboard the Titanic, for they shall be filled with gratitude, and gratitude is the mother of all prayer.

A Nose Tickling Feather

A study has shown it's not the smell of roses or home-baked bread that is most pleasing to a sizable portion of American males. Rather, it's the smell of a new automobile! Accordingly, chemists of the Orlandi Company of Long Island, New York, recently were able to create a synthetic "new car" smell. Now, musty used cars can immediately be made more appealing with one spray of a can.

Think of the possibilities if the Orlandi chemists could recreate the smell of a honeymoon! Old and musty marriages could instantly be made romantic and exciting. Until that heavily scented odor of love and passion can be chemically synthesized, however, what can you do to re-romance your love, work and life?

Nose Tickling Feather II

According to Chicago's Smell and Taste Treatment Research Foundation, the smell of apples makes a room seem larger. Barbecue smoke, on the other hand, makes a room seem smaller. The next time your world seems too cramped and limiting, try eating an apple, inhaling deeply the aroma of each bite.

Furthermore, it's not only the odor of barbecue smoke that shrinks the size of your world. Consider, for example, the possible effects of the following smells: nationalism, religious superiority, racial and sexual discrimination. Perhaps an apple a day can keep the devil of parochialism away.

Also, ask yourself what your prayers smell like: apples or barbecue smoke?

~ Chapter 3 ~

Nine
Feathers on
Religion

Eaten Alive by the Saints

To live like a feather on the Wind involves being lighthearted even in the face of the often serious and constricting world of religion. Sometimes that means not getting bound up in the "business" of religion; sometimes it requires not being blindly overzealous at the expense of loving; sometimes it calls for not taking yourself too seriously, adding a touch of humor or playfulness to lighten up the religious search.

The Rumanians have a proverb that I love: "Before you can find God, you are eaten by the saints." Life is a hide-and-seek game with God. From early childhood till the moment we close our eyes in death, we are looking for our hidden God. And there's no shortage of experts eager to show us how to find God, *their* God. I don't know about you, but I've been disappointed time and again with the God that has been shown to me by experts. Personally, I prefer the God that Jesus spoke about, the God which he had undoubtedly found. Further, he told us that he was the Way to God and that if we followed him we too would find God. However, it's an old problem—I mean, finding God—so don't feel bad if you're still looking.

As you daily try your best to walk in the footsteps of Jesus, you find a crowd of pious people walking the same path. They're often a serious bunch, deadly intent on being "fully alive," as Jesus promised: "I have come that you might have life and have it to the full" (Jn. 10: 10). I call these people "the saints"—that's what Christ's followers were called in the early Church. But the Rumanians were right: Before you can find God, the saints really do eat you up!

The saints love to rush up and give you a big hug, beaming over with joy and love. Frequently, however, they're complete strangers; I mean, I've never even seen some of them before. They say, "Give

me a hug" or "Could I have a hug?" Now, I come from a warm and loving Irish family; affectionate expressions were common in our clan. I'm not a frigid person, but I often freeze when the "Saints Come Marching In." I don't like to give an expression of love as intimate as an embrace to someone I hardly know because for me it cheapens both the symbol and the reality expressed by the symbol.

I find the affection and warmth of today's Church to be refreshing. And if I've spent a day on retreat with someone I've just met and at least had an opportunity to share some thoughts and feelings and a common experience of the presence of Christ, a hug feels natural and fitting. But complete strangers who want "Christian" hugs is for me an experience of being nibbled upon. I guess I haven't reached that level of holiness where I'm so swept up in the mystery of God that there are no strangers left on earth. As I said, I'm still looking for God.

The saints have other ways of eating away at you. As I try time and again to make my shoes fit inside Christ's footprints, I find that they don't take me to church and prayer gatherings so much as to bars and to dinners with sinners. I say sinners—not that I think they are, but that they think they are—since they have chosen to be non-religious. From my reading of the Gospels, it seems that Jesus didn't care much for the company of the saints of his day. While he chose the companionship of outcasts and religious rejects to bring them a new lease on life, maybe he also wanted to save himself from being eaten alive by the saints.

You Just Gotta Save Christianity!

In the 1935 movie *The Crusades* the character played by Loretta Young says to Richard the Lionhearted, "You just gotta save Christianity, Richard, you gotta!" In every age since the death of Jesus, people have heard that same urgent call, "You just gotta save Christianity," and have rushed out their front doors on a crusade. Today is no different than a thousand years ago: the need to save Christianity launches fresh crusades almost daily.

Historically, crusades, both large and small, have been deployed to "save" Christianity from: the Jews, Roman Catholics, Protestants, Moslems, free-thinkers and a host of others. Crusades, private and official, have targeted such threats to the faith as science, the waltz, medicine, the printing press, rock 'n' roll, motion pictures, television and _____ *(fill in the blank)*.

Since the Second Vatican Council, scores of eager volunteers have felt that they "gotta" save the Church and Christianity. These Vatican Vigilantes jam their bishops' mailboxes—and the Pope's—with "sightings" of heresy. They are disturbed by certain statements in the pastor's sermon, by girl servers, inclusive language or microscopic changes in the ritual of the Mass.

It's ironic that if Christianity's "gotta be" saved from anything it's from Christians! The paradox is that those who try to protect Christianity from heresy do so by committing heresy. Jesus called his disciples to love and respect one another and their enemies. Yet in their passion to save Christianity—and often out of their fears—disciples of Christ have attacked, tortured and burned "heretics" at the stake. Jesus said we were to love our enemies, yet zealous crusaders malign, accuse and condemn those they view as the

enemies of the Church.

If you feel impelled to save Christianity by launching or joining a moral crusade, remember how Jesus felt about them. The first crusade was launched by Pope Peter I when he drew his sword in the Garden of Gethsemani to save Jesus. Jesus, however, told him, "Peter, put away your sword. You don't understand; God has other plans. Don't get in the way of them" (See Mt. 26: 52).

Let us not be fearful about the fate of the Church or the world. Instead, let us strive to live in the spirit of Easter's promise. Jesus promised his fearful disciples that he would be with them always, even to the earth's last gasp. It was God and not the sword that saved Jesus; so too it will be God that saves Christianity. Belief in the abiding presence of Jesus is an important part of any good spirituality. If that belief doesn't calm your anxious heart, then pray over and over that powerful two-word message of the angel at the tomb on the first Easter morning: "Fear not."

Onward Christian Soldiers
—to Wichita

Only a few men were at the bar of the Hotel Carey, Wichita's finest saloon, on the chilly winter morning of December 27, 1890. They were bracing themselves against the cold when, out of the blue, the bar was "invaded" by a hatchet-swinging Mrs. Carry Nation. The notorious Kansas temperance leader sent the bar's customers diving for cover as she began to smash away at whiskey bottles, glasses and the large crystal chandelier. The black-bonneted crusader against the evils of drink shouted, "Peace on earth, good will to men," to the sound of smashing glass. By the time the dust had settled, the temperance tornado had also destroyed a fifteen hundred dollar mirror and the large plate glass covering a huge nude painting of Cleopatra. When the police arrived at the hotel and arrested Mrs. Nation, she serenaded them—all the way to the jail—with chorus after chorus of "Am I a Soldier of the Cross?"

No doubt Carry Nation must have seen herself as a soldier of the cross. How else could such a "good Christian woman" do so much damage to another's property? The song she sang in the paddy wagon on the way to the Wichita jail is itself a contradiction. How is it possible to be a soldier of the cross, if the cross is the very symbol of a non-violent response to evil? Certainly in the first few centuries after the Resurrection, when military duty was itself an obstacle to being a Christian, one could not be a "soldier of the cross."

Each time we are tempted to imitate the behavior of Carry Nation, even if our wrath only uses words as weapons, we might consider a different version of that old hymn about being a disciple of the cross.

Regardless of how great the evil that we oppose, can we ever employ violent means to attack that evil and still be true followers of Jesus? Folklore calls us to fight fire with fire, but the Gospel calls us to fight fire with love, with peaceful, non-violent resistance.

A hundred years ago in Wichita, those opposed to the use of alcohol must have applauded Carry's wrathful destruction of the city's finest bar. Many contemporary Christians would nod with approval at news headlines about the destruction of Wichita's abortion clinic. While we personally might not engage in violent physical attacks on what we consider to be moral evils, whenever we rejoice in or condone such un-crosslike behavior, we share in it. If we wish to be true disciples of Christ, let us not by action or applause support any violent resolution to evil.

Does your spirituality include a place for violence in word or deed, or even a hidden place for violent thoughts? If it does, ask yourself if it is truly a Christian spirituality, at least one to which Jesus would be willing to lend his name.

Blest Are the Unequal

Wasn't Jesus guilty of discrimination when he said, "Unless you become as little children, you cannot enter the reign of God"? Is not his denial of admission to adults a violation of equal rights? His call for us to become like children has, in the hands of spiritual writers and preachers, given birth to a host of romantic interpretations, which might be summed up: we should be innocent, playful and trusting. While these are admirable virtues, there is some question about what Jesus really meant. Besides, the question remains: Isn't his restricting entrance to heaven still an act of discrimination?

Today's battle for equal rights began long ago when commoners demanded equality with kings and nobles under the law. In time, society has seen legal equality granted to all white males, then to women, and finally in the second half of the twentieth century to African-Americans and other minorities. Women, who have been discriminated against for centuries in business, state and church, are on the verge of full equality. There is still work to be done, but today equal rights under the law are guaranteed for the vast majority of persons, regardless of their sex, sexual orientation, race, religion or ethnic heritage. As a result, the words of Jesus about who will enter the Kingdom are most disturbing since he says that the age of God is open only to those who are eager to have "unequal" rights!

In Near Eastern culture at the time of Jesus, children had *zero* rights! Children occupied the lowest level of the social ladder. They had no legal rights, no say in family matters, no power or control over their lives. They even had little or no voice about whom they would marry; this decision belonged to their parents, who frequently pledged them to

marriage at an early age. It seemed shocking in his day that Jesus should promise the Kingdom only to those who were in last place, the poor in power. The paradox of discipleship is that it requires tirelessly laboring for justice and equality for all, while at the same time seeking for yourself a lowly and "unequal" place.

Cardinal Merry de Val, who lived at the start of the twentieth century, prayed daily for this privileged, "lowly" place wherein is hidden the door to heaven. This reflection concludes with an abridged form of his daily prayer, his Litany of Humility. If you're looking for the hidden entrance to the Kingdom of God, you might want to consider making his truly feather-light prayer part of your prayers:

> O Jesus, meek and humble of heart,
>> deliver me from the desire
>> of being esteemed, of being loved,
>> of being extolled, of being honored,
>> of being praised and preferred to others,
>> of being consulted and approved.
> O Jesus, meek and humble of heart,
>> deliver me from the fear of
>> being humiliated, forgotten, ridiculed,
>> wronged, despised, rebuked and suspected.
> Jesus, grant me the grace to desire that
>> others may be loved more than I,
>> more esteemed, chosen, praised
>> and preferred to me in everything.
> Jesus, grant me the grace to desire that
>> others become holier than I,
>> provided that I may become
>> as holy as I should.

Sin Taxes

The first months of every year have two things in common: taxes and Lent. At first glance they may appear unrelated, but they're really kissing cousins. Your IRS payment and Lent both deal with debts, one owed to the government and the other to God. We acknowledge the second kind of debt when we *pray*, "Forgive us our debts as we forgive...." The first debt, of course, we address when we *pay*. This meditation, however, is not just for the early months of the year; to paraphrase that famous saying, "Lent and Taxes are always with us."

Once upon a time, this unlikely couple was actually formally married. Centuries ago in England, for example, there was a church tax called the Cradle Crown. As a form of penance, it was a tax levied upon a priest who had fathered a child and had a live-in companion. Lent would be the perfect time for the Church to restore her medieval system of sin taxes. That happy reunion of Lent and taxes would be a great blessing to the Church, which in almost every diocese is having to cut back on services because of a lack of funds. Perhaps the solution to your parish's financial problems isn't tithing but sin taxes!

Consider the implications of the restoration of sin taxes for a financially strapped Vatican—or your parish. Such a taxation would resolve the distasteful problem of sermons on money, not to mention being a more realistic approach toward human nature. The following are but a few taxable sins and their suggested annual fee:

Living together but not married:	$200.00
Adultery or fornication:	$200.00
Celibate yet sexually active:	$250.00
Divorced but remarried:	$200.00
Missing Mass frequently:	$165.00

Dirty jokes and/or foul language: $100.00
Gossip or slander: $150.00
Cheating on your income tax: $ 50.00

Sin, like alcohol, is here to stay. So why not tax it? Besides, whoever said sin was free? A recent survey revealed that eight out of ten Americans believe that some day they must answer for—pay for—their sins!

We can ask, however, if such a belief is good Christian theology. Do we not believe that Jesus paid our sin taxes, that he completely wiped away all our debts? Likewise, as in the parable of the Prodigal Son, Jesus taught that God forgives unconditionally and instantly. For Jesus, God's forgiveness requires no repentance, no crawling on your knees, begging for pardon. His practice of freely pardoning sin was radical and revolutionary. Nowhere in all the Gospel stories about pardon does Jesus require remorse or even sorrow from those he forgave.

If all our debts have been forgiven, what then is the purpose of doing penance for our sins? One answer is suggested in the behavior of the village whore who washed Jesus' feet and dried them with her hair. That kind of repentance is the expression of extravagant love surging from the knowledge of how much is the debt we have been forgiven.

To return to our theme of sin and taxes, a debt-free repentance is more a state of remembrance than of reparation. It's an act of recalling our sinfulness so as to "go overboard" in our loving. Although Lent's liturgical color is purple for penance, we might better see it as the purple passion of great loving.

Is Being a Christian Dangerous to Your Freedom?

While Baptism is "good medicine," it can also have certain dangerous side effects, like slavery! In *Rascals in Paradise*, James Michener looks at slavery in the South Pacific in the late 1870s. While slavery was dying in North America, it was just beginning in the islands of the Pacific. The Civil War had disrupted the world cotton trade, and the growing of cotton was shifting to Australia. Workers were needed for the new Pacific cotton industry as well as the region's new sugar plantations. It is estimated that over fifty sailing vessels were involved in the trade of *blackbirding*, the polite name for kidnapping natives to be sold as slaves!

As with African slave trade, Pacific blackbirding included all the horrors humans can inflict upon one another. A striking difference, however, occurred in the new slave trade. The natives sought as potential slaves were those whom missionaries had baptized as Christians! Entire Christian congregations were kidnapped and sold into slavery. Blackbirding targeted baptized island natives because the docility taught to them by missionaries made them better slave workers in the cotton fields.

Particularly for Americans, freedom is a hallowed life quality. It, therefore, might be a good idea to take a Freedom Test to examine any dangerous side effects of your Baptism. Here are some freedom questions:

1. Does Baptism into Christ make you more or less independent than others?
2. Does your Christian faith, with its emphasis on obedience to authority, make you a docile sheep who is more easily led—or does it inspire you to live in the glorious freedom of the

children of God?

3. Does your faith make you question what authority figures tell you—or what you learn from newspapers and television?

4. When it comes to making decisions and determining moral values, do you think for yourself or turn such choices over to experts, relatives or friends?

Propaganda's hypnotic power lies in the constant repetition of any information, whether it be true or false. Propaganda works best on those who are docile and law-abiding, who have a lust for strong leaders. The child in us is easily swayed by propaganda and is easily manipulated by media-ganda and pulpit-ganda. We are even more easily seduced to become docile sheep when we are spoken to from "above," be it from the lectern, pulpit or the Oval Office of the White House.

Like the 4th of July, Easter is a feast for non-sheep. It is a celebration of those who refuse to be enslaved in body, mind or heart. As a closing test of your freedom, ponder this quotation from the gifted author Graham Greene: "As a Roman Catholic I thank God for heretics. Heresy is only another word for freedom of thought."

The Dangers of Dry Cleaning and Confession

According to Debra Dadd's book *Nontoxic, Natural, & Earthwise*, dry-cleaned clothing is a serious source of home pollution! Each time you return from the cleaners with a garment in its plastic bag, you bring a toxic health problem into your home. The process of removing stains from specially cleaned garments involves the use of strong solvent chemicals. Dadd cautions that your dry-cleaned clothing should be removed from the plastic covers as soon as you get home. To ensure the evaporation of all the harmful chemicals, the clothing should be hung in a well-ventilated area, ideally outdoors. In cold weather this could take more than a week, a bit less time in warm weather. It appears that the last state of the garment—being clean—is worse than the first—being dirty.

Jesus expressed a similar environmental concern about going to confession. His caution, found in Luke's Gospel, tells of an unclean spirit who left a soul and then couldn't find anywhere to reside. So the spirit decided, "I'll go back where I came from." It returned and found the house all swept and nicely cleaned. It then went out and found seven other evil spirits, far worse than itself, and returned to its original dwelling. Jesus said, "The result is that the last state of the soul was worse than the first" (Lk. 11: 26).

Confessing our sins as a way to reform our lives is as hazardous as bringing home freshly dry-cleaned garments. Nothing is more dangerous than confessing a sin, promising never to commit it again and going home with a freshly cleaned soul. A good confession creates a vacuum which only invites an invasion by spirits more evil than those driven out. To sweep clean our souls of sin is not enough, regardless of how deep

our sorrow and contrition.

To repent of such common household sins as the habit of gossiping is good, but it can be dangerous if we do not replace the old habit with a new one. For example, instead of being the local broadcaster of others' failings and mistakes, we can become their press agent. Replace the habit of gossiping with a pattern of praising others, speaking of their gifts and talents. Be prepared, however, that such new patterns, like freeing your dry cleaning of its toxic residue, will take time. Developing a new habit will take at least a week, longer if you don't pursue it with passion.

Do Debra Dadd's anxieties about the dangers of dry-cleaned clothes seem excessive to you? How serious is the danger of those chemical odors that are nearly impossible to smell? Can the same not also be said of Jesus' concerns about something so positive as sweeping clean our inner-houses of evil?

When we feel the need to go to confession, we should take some time to consider our homework after we have been reconciled. Are we willing to do the necessary environmental work of replacing our sinful, negative behavior with a positive one? If we're too busy or do not feel inclined to do so, perhaps it's better not to go to confession! If we do fill the newly cleansed empty space with good thoughts and good practices, then great things can happen in our souls—and in the world!

Laugh, But Only at Risk to Your Soul!

While laughter can be an expression of Easter joy, be careful if you want to receive Holy Communion this Sunday! Although mirth and laughter are often recommended for good health, they can be lethal to your religious life. Medical evidence indicates that laughter releases the body's natural pain killers; it can also get you thrown out of Church! Laughter, if brief and proper—perhaps as a response to something said in the homily—is acceptable to most people in solemn church services. At other times in our worship, overt demonstrations of joy are proper only if they are expressed in ancient foreign words such as "alleluia."

While joy is the litmus test for the presence of the Spirit of God, we tend to cautiously express it in prayer and worship—and for a good reason. It is not by accident that our faith is somber and serious, for who wants to be excommunicated? An ordinance from the Second Council of Constance in 1418 states, "If any cleric or monk speaks jocular words, such as provoke laughter, let him be anathema." Keep in mind that *anathema* means formal ecclesiastical excommunication! What's interesting to me as a cleric is that the Church condemned a priest or monk who had caused others to laugh not simply at Mass, but anywhere!

Thank God that in my life I've known monks and priests who risked excommunication and made me laugh. Thank God that I've known ministers and even bishops who have made my life more joyful by their humor. I'm not sure who will make up the agenda of the next ecumenical council, but I propose a write-in campaign for one particular item. We could petition the Vatican to ask the world's bishops to

retract the Council of Constance's edict of excommunication for laughter. Priests, bishops and even the pope then could be free to be more joyful. As spiritual leaders of the community they could set a new attitude for everyone in the Church. A pope or bishop who could make us laugh with a good joke or humorous story would do wonders for the health of the Church.

Of course, a lack of humor is not confined to the Catholic Church. Other Christian denominations and other religious traditions are no less staid and somber. If a heresy has ever crept into religions and hid away, it has to be the heresy that holiness and humor, laughter and sanctity, are opposed to one another. How sad that our religion, our relationship with God, must be solemn and serious. Is the taboo against laughter because we want our faith to be "respectable" so it will be taken seriously? Regardless of the reason, spice up your prayer and your life lived in communion with God with laughter and good humor.

Forget the Council of Constance and celebrate Easter joy by indulging in a good laugh. Let your resurrection prayers be smiles at strangers on the street, or passing on a good joke. Then, celebrate the joyous victory of Christ over death by going to Holy Communion with a smile on your face.

The Love Boat?

In Norfolk, Virginia, recently, 103 vacationers eagerly climbed aboard the cruise ship *World Discoverer*, having purchased tickets for a "Cruise to Nowhere." The passengers had no idea of the voyage's destination or its ports of call. A few miles out of port, however, the pleasure ship ran into fog, developed generator trouble and had to be towed back into Norfolk.

Sadly, that kind of cruise happens all the time— not as a vacation but as a way of life! How many of us have no idea where we are going? Do you, like the people aboard the *World Discoverer*, leave your destination in the hands of others? Those who fail to be their own captains soon find they are sailing in the fog. We each have a choice to either create our future or to become a victim of events and history.

In religion, politics and daily life, do you prefer not to know where you're going and thus leave that choice to others? If so, remember how the "Cruise to Nowhere" was exactly what those 103 passengers got for their money.

~ Chapter 4 ~

Ten Feathers on
Prayer

A Prayer's Life Span

I have a couple of shoe boxes filled with old cards and letters that I treasure. As an average American, I receive close to 600 letters a year, most of which end up in my waste basket. There are, however, notes and letters from persons I love that are too precious to be thrown away. I'd guess that you also have such memorial mail stored away in your home. My old shoe boxes are like safety deposit boxes since they contain what I cherish most in life: expressions of love and friendship. Whenever I place a letter in my box or take one out to reread it, I can't help but wonder if God also has an old shoe box.

That question sparks a similar question, "What happens to my prayers after I pray them?" The life expectancy of a prayer is usually thought to be as brief as the time required to pray it. But what if a prayer is eternal?

Think of our prayers as if they were mail. Our daily mail contains form letters, advertisements and personal correspondence. I sort through my mail and usually read my personal mail first, sometimes saving a special letter till last to enjoy it like dessert. As for my junk mail, most of it goes unopened straight into the "circular file." I wonder if God sorts through prayers in a similar way.

A prayer can be like a form letter if it's prayed only with our lips and not with our hearts. Prayers also can be like begging letters in which we plead some personal cause or need. Others are like letters of recommendation wherein we promote another's needs. Finally, some prayers resemble "thank you" notes or love letters. For prayers to be eternal—the kind that God might safely store away—we need to be more attentive and wholehearted when we pray.

Since we pray in and through Christ and since

Christ is eternally one with God, it only seems logical that our prayers would be eternal. Furthermore, we shouldn't be anxious about our prayers lacking poetic style because making them sincere and praying them one with Christ must make them awesomely attractive to God. If we really want God to consider our prayers beautiful enough to keep them eternally in a special shoe box, we need to pay careful attention to what we are doing each time we pray. We need to invest our prayers with a real and unquenchable devotion. Each time we do that, our prayers become light as a feather that floats with infinite ease above the clouds to God.

Hitting the Bull's Eye

A Japanese soldier who defended Osaka testified that the anti-aircraft guns in his area fired mostly blanks in the last months of World War II! According to an article in the *Knoxville News-Sentinel*, even though ammunition was in short supply, the military didn't want to be criticized for not trying to defend their people. Even when real shells were used, the Japanese soldiers realized that they could not reach the high-flying B-29 bombers. Those soldiers risked their lives just to keep up the appearance of defending their homeland. While admiring their courage, we might question the common sense of such a course of action.

That same need to be seen as being faithful to our duties, the importance of keeping up appearances and pretending that everything is normal, has a lot of us shooting blanks! That kind of "pretending" in marriage, or any life-commitment, can be dangerous to our health. It can make us sick in body and mind. At the very least, it's a sad waste of time, energy and life. When, like the Osaka defenders, we pretend that everything is normal, we make a lot of noise shooting blanks, merely keeping busy instead of honestly facing reality. The purpose of keeping up appearances is based on the notion of doing one's duty. Yet is our real duty to pretend all is well or to acknowledge the truth of a situation?

The modern-day parable of the defenders of Osaka should challenge each of us to explore our relationships, our work and particularly our prayer and worship for any wasted energy in maintaining appearances. The defenders of Osaka were at best only halfhearted in their duty, even when they fired live ammunition at enemy planes which were out of the range of their shells. How much of our worship is similarly halfhearted, simply "doing our duty"?

Meal prayers, morning and evening prayers, prayers at meetings—all prayers—should be carefully examined to see if they are real. Our personal or communal prayers spoken without thought and feeling are blanks; they are empty and hollow. Oh, they may give the appearance of devotion and reliance on God, but they are without substance.

Furthermore, prayers are like wasted ammunition even when said with attention and thought but without faith and a deep-seated devotion, since they will never reach their target—God. Making the sign of the cross, the taking of holy water upon entering a church, reverence shown to the Blessed Sacrament—these and other wordless rituals need to be done with mindfulness and faith. A good rule of thumb for both hunting and praying is: Only shoot real ammunition at a close target—or use enough "gun powder" to reach the mark.

Which Way to Face
When Praying

Orthodox Muslims face Mecca whenever they pray, and devout Jews once faced Jerusalem while praying. As a Christian, which direction do you face when you pray?

In *A Trip to the Mountains*, Annie Dillard writes about the customs of the Native American Indians of our Northwest. She tells of a teenager named John Ireland who in the summer of 1872 visited an Indian village near Bellingham Bay, about 90 miles north of Seattle. Ireland observed the Skagit Indians, who were Catholics, as they gathered to pray. They formed a circle with everyone facing inward. Then they all made the sign of the cross and began to pray. Ireland recalled a previous visit to the Nooksack Indians, who were Methodists, while they were at prayer. The Nooksacks likewise formed a circle, but they faced outward when they prayed. Naturally, the young man wondered about the implications of these two different positions of prayer.

It's important to face in toward the center when praying. Such "centering prayer," directed to God who is at the heart of each of us, at the heart of the community and the world, helps us balance and find our true ground. At the same time, good prayer always faces outward, regardless of which direction the body is facing. Good prayer mirrors the prayer of Jesus which was truly encompassing. His prayer embraced not only those who were near, but all peoples. His mission was not to save his soul or those of his followers but to save the world.

Our bodily position at prayer has a powerful influence upon us: the way we hold our hands, if we kneel or stand, sit or prostrate ourselves. Consider

what the implications would be if the next time you pray in a group everyone were to form a circle and face outward. You might first face inward as you pray for the needs of those within the circle. Then, after a brief pause, turn and face outward, praying for the needs of the whole Church and for all who live on our small planet.

You can face outward without actually changing your physical position. In both personal and family prayer, after praying for your needs and those of your family, you can direct your prayer outward. With your heart in a global position, pray for the needs of all the different peoples of this earth, as well as the needs of the earth herself.

A global prayer position can also be expressed by standing to pray at the window of your bedroom. As you look out your window, pray for all those who live in houses you can see and then beyond them for home-dwellers throughout the world—and for the homeless! A similar gesture at the end of family prayer would be for one member to go to the front door, open it and pray for the needs of your neighborhood, city, country and the world.

If we are truly "Catholic"—that is, *universal*—Christians, should not our style of prayer be global and world-encompassing? Another way to express Jesus' definition of how the world would recognize his disciples might be: "By this will all know that you are my disciples, in that when you pray, you always face outward" (see Jn. 13: 35).

Bless Us, O Lord,
and These Thy Soul Gifts

Because of heightened consciousness about proper diet, many of us have become label readers. We carefully read food labels to see if the contents are free of fat, cholesterol, salt, sugar or any artificial ingredients. According to recent studies, the number one concern of Americans is their weight! As a result, eating—or non-eating—is serious business for us. If you take eating earnestly and are concerned about what you put into your body, then meal prayers should be particularly important to you.

In all cultures, eating has been viewed as a sacred act. For Christians, whose central religious act is that of remembering the last dinner eaten by Jesus, every meal should be a sacred leftover of that meal. Meal prayers give us a wonderful opportunity to recall that holy heritage. Yet praying at mealtimes is rapidly becoming a religious relic. What once was an absolute family requirement has become relegated to special occasions.

Perhaps part of the reason for the disappearance of family meal prayers is the disappearance of family meals! It has been estimated that only three out of ten American families eat together even as often as once a week! Family rituals like prayers before meals encourage each family member to remember to pray. However, whether eating alone or with others, let's not let this wonderful and ancient tradition of prayer fade away.

Praying before eating requires some discipline since we're usually hungry and eager to begin the meal. On the other hand, no discipline is required to pray when we are in danger; prayer at such times is almost spontaneous. If, however, we were aware of

the perils involved in eating, we might also have no difficulty remembering to pray before a meal. For Eskimo Indian holy men, to eat any meal is considered a dangerous activity because it involves the eating of souls!

Aware that all animals and plants are alive and therefore have souls, Eskimos approach food with great reverence. To eat caribou, deer or seal is to also eat the creature's soul, an action that holds dire consequences if done blindly. Today, we who do not hunt for our food—other than on the shelves of the local supermarket—can easily become blind to who or what we're eating. Wouldn't our consciousness skyrocket if the main course at supper were our pet cat or dog? Of all peoples, we Christians, who dine upon the body and blood of Christ, should be aware of "soul food."

If you have abandoned meal prayers or say them as if on automatic pilot, the next time you come to the table remember the Eskimos. Pause in silence before you eat. Be grateful that the beef or beans have given up their souls, their life, that you might live. As you pause in gratitude to honor the Source of all gifts—as well as the gift of the souls of the potato, fish or pork on the plate before you—dedicate yourself to pouring forth your soul for the life of others. In your willingness to give your life for others, you pray the best of all meal prayers.

A Prayer Comb

What do you carry in your pocket or purse that's like a church bell? Car keys, change, a handkerchief, billfold or compact? Perhaps the best answer to the riddle is your comb! The next time you use your comb, like a church bell, let it call you to prayer! "Prayer?" you might ask. "As I'm combing my hair?" While not usually associated with prayer, daily grooming is an ideal "church bell" since no one neglects it. Such comb-prayer is not only ideal for our busy lives— since we seem to never have time for prayer—it's also an *ancient* prayer form!

Hair combs have been found in six-thousand-year-old Egyptian tombs, and their design hasn't changed much since they were first invented. A comb still resembles a row of teeth, the name coming from the old word *gombhos* which means "teeth." Historians believe the first combs were dried backbones of large fish. Such fish-combs are still used today by remote tribes in Africa.

A lost relic of Christian liturgical prayer is the ritual of a priest's prayer while combing his hair in the sacristy before Vespers! Combs have also been discovered among the artifacts in the catacombs of the early Christian martyrs. Since that was where the faithful gathered to reenact the Last Supper and pray, it is quite possible that combs had a liturgical function. Before you dismiss such a weird, "hairy," idea, ask yourself why the earliest stained-glass windows included images of combs?

I'm not a liturgical scholar or archeologist, but I am fascinated with how our ancestors prayed. I propose the following theory about hair prayer, not as an explanation to the mystery of combs and worship, but as a new way to pray. Grooming, even our custom of carrying a comb or hairbrush, is an

activity overripe with possibility as a new way to "pray always." Early Christians did not restrict their prayer to when they went to church, since they didn't have churches—their homes were their places of worship. While they had set times of prayer, they also were eager to pray *always* as Jesus had encouraged them. Furthermore, they lived in a culture hostile to their faith and so daily lived in fear and in danger of death.

Each knock at the door could have meant prison or torture, and so an early Christian's comb was a marvelous reminder of the words of Jesus about how all-embracing is God's protection of them. "All will hate you because of me, yet not a hair of your head will be harmed. By your patient endurance you will save your lives" (Lk. 21: 17-19). It would have been a small step to invest one's daily grooming with those words as a reminder of God's constant care.

Today, a pocket comb and handkerchief are usually among the objects found in a man's pockets. Women carry combs or hairbrushes in their purses. In effect we carry a constant reminder of a way to pray always. Each time you comb your hair as part of your daily grooming, recall God's loving care for you. In times of fear or danger hold your comb in your hand as a sacramental and pray the words of Jesus, "In very truth, even the hairs of your head are counted! Fear nothing, then. You are worth more than a flock of sparrows" (Lk. 12: 7).

A Waste of Time?

Life is not so much composed of grand moments as small, endless events that seem insignificant. If you add up all those events, however, they amount to a considerable part of your lifetime. Studies show, for example, that average Americans spend about one year of their lives simply searching for lost belongings! A few minutes here, a few there, but over a lifetime they do add up. Or take meetings. During an average lifetime, a person spends around three years sitting in meetings. If you're in pastoral ministry, it may be closer to thirty years—or at least it feels like that at times.

Dan Sperling, in *Study in Time's A-Wasting*, also suggests that we spend five years out of life waiting in line and eight months opening junk mail. It's not easy to come up with something you can do to transform all that wasted time opening junk mail, but the five years waiting in line—ah, that's got possibilities! Whenever we are forced to wait, we are provided with an opportunity to rest a bit from the hectic pace of life. That time can also be used to examine more closely the world around us that usually whizzes by like a video film run on fast-forward.

What usually prevents us from enjoying these unexpected "pause" moments is being on a schedule, a very tight schedule, that has very little allowance for delays. It is the schedule's dictator-voice inside that creates the turmoil in our hearts, that can turn a once pleasant day into a visit to hell. Our term *schedule* comes from the word for the paper on which was written the program for the day. It's an old Latin word meaning "a small leaf." Since parchment was made from papyrus leaves, it's easy to understand the name. However, the original Greek word from which *schedule* came means "a splinter of wood." When we allow

our schedules to cause us to become upset, as unexpected delays force us to wait, then a schedule becomes like a splinter of wood under a fingernail.

The next time you feel that splinter under your fingernail or stuck in your heart, pull it out. Instead of being forced to wait, realize that you are invited to patiently pause in life and enjoy what's going on around you. Patience is not an exercise in grim endurance but rather a creative use of the time you are asked to wait. Furthermore, some of the events and commitments on your daily schedule may be able to be bumped. Things you thought *must* be done today can often wait till tomorrow. With such a feather-light attitude you can not only relieve some stress, you can enrich your life.

When you are forced to wait, don't throw away any of that five years of life by becoming upset and angry. It's such a waste of the precious commodity we possess so briefly: Life. And if you have to wait in traffic or for someone you are supposed to meet and can't think of anything creative to do with all that "wasted" waiting time, why not use it to pray? What a wonderful opportunity to add five more years of prayer to your life!

Swiss Cheese Spirituality

Cardinal Richard James Cushing of Boston once told journalist Harry Reasoner about the time a young priest came to visit him. Worried and anxious, the young man told the old cardinal, "Your Excellency, I am losing my faith." According to Reasoner, Cardinal Cushing answered, "Meaning no disrespect to your intellectual attainments, Father, but you and I are much too dumb to lose our faith. Great heretics like Martin Luther lose their faith. You and I just get bored!"

Boredom is like Swiss cheese. It's a condition in which dullness and drab repetition bore holes into our faith and love. Life and vitality can then easily drain out from those holes. A good farmer keeps a vigilant eye for corn borers, the larva of a moth that feeds on corn. If we don't want to lose our faith by having it filled with holes, we must watch for church borers.

Since all ritual is repetition and all religion is remembering the past, dullness can easily become the occupational disease of religious people. While children, being more honest, often complain that "church is boring," adults deny this reality, at least to their children. Because Mass is frequently like Swiss cheese, we insist that it be as swift as possible. Lengthy sporting events, concerts and motion pictures, which are experienced as enjoyable and alive, however, are another matter.

Both in public worship and in personal prayer, change is the best anti-boredom treatment. Creative innovation and doing something as if it were the first —or the last—time is how we keep bores out of our marriages or our religion. The Risen Christ set the tone for creative prayer, life and making love: "See, I make all things new" (Rev. 21: 5). A new covenant, a

new commandment, a new way of life, is at the heart of the Good News. If the new covenant is to remain constantly new, it must be constantly revitalized and energized. The same treatment is necessary in our personal covenants with God, each other and our daily work. People fall out of love with God as they do with each other—from boredom!

Destiny—and God—have set us down on the hot stove top of history with orders to "make all things new." Those are papal orders as well! Good Pope John XXIII, when opening the Vatican Council, gave this reason for calling it together: "Today the Church is witnessing a crisis underway in society...society is on the verge of a new era...a task of great importance awaits the Church...of bringing the modern world into life-giving contact with the Gospel" (*Humanae Salutis*).

Regardless of our religious faith, or lack of it, we have been given a task of great importance: to fertilize the new world that's a-birthing with the evergreen newness of the Good News. The world, however, will only listen to a vibrant, interesting, enjoyable and creatively dynamic Gospel. News that is boring and dull, with no hope of change, can never be called *Good* News.

Long-Distance Prayer

Halford Luccock, a Yale professor in the late 1930s, spoke about the danger of becoming "anniversary Christians." While he stressed the important role of remembrance in the Judeo-Christian tradition, he also felt that we Christians have a "memorial complex." Luccock said that religion, like a marriage, easily becomes nothing more than the celebration of anniversaries, remembrances of what long ago was exciting and full of life.

With our Liturgical Year of feasts which celebrate the anniversaries of events in the life of Christ, his mother and the disciples, we Christians can slip into a holy, once-upon-a-time-and-long-ago religion. If we are anniversary keepers, then it's easy to see God's dynamic involvement in the world as happening only long ago in some faraway land and not just as truly in our times.

Anniversary Christians, when they pray, also have problems making good connections with God. Since much of our prayer is conversation with God, it so easily can become long-distance prayer.

There's a story about former Israeli Prime Minister Menachem Begin's visit to Washington during the Carter administration. Seated in the Oval Office of the White House, Prime Minister Begin asked President Carter about the three telephones on the president's desk.

"The white phone goes to Plains, Georgia, so I can keep track of my brother Billy. The red phone, of course, is the hot line to Moscow, which gives me instant communication with the Russians. And the gold phone—it's a direct line to God!"

"How much does that cost?" asked Begin.

"Ten thousand dollars a month," Carter is said to have replied, "but, Mr. Prime Minister, it's worth

every cent."

Some time later, Carter visited Israel and sat with Begin in his office. Seeing three telephones on his desk, Carter asked, "Why do you have three phones?"

"Well, the white phone is a hot line to Cairo, Egypt. The red phone is my direct line to Parliament, and my gold phone is a direct line to God!"

Carter asked, "What does your line to God cost?"

"Ten cents," Begin replied. "It's a local call!"

The shrinkage of daily prayer among upper- and middle-class Americans could be due to the fact that they think of their conversations with God as long-distance calls! This attitude is revealed in a recent poll which shows that a large number of people pray only in church. Could the reason for limiting prayer to Sundays be because the rates are cheaper on weekends?

The style and shape of our prayers reveal whether we believe that God is near or distant from both our lives and daily world. When our prayers are stiff and formal, devoid of expressions found in daily speech, it can indicate that we consider God to be remote. When we ask others, especially professional religious, to pray to God for our intentions, it's a sign that we feel only they have what we lack: a direct line!

Each of us, saint or sinner, is like Prime Minister Begin. Each of us has at our fingertips a gold phone. We can speak directly to God anytime we need to. And the good news is: It's a local call!

Soup de Jour

French influence in cooking and foods is considerable. Take, for example, our name on menus for the soup of the day, *Soup de Jour*, and the name for a place to eat, a *restaurant*. The latter was first used, in plural form, to designate the eating establishment of a Paris soup vender named Boulanger. The sign over his shop read *Restaurants*, meaning "restoratives," for the hot soups and broths available inside. In a short period of time his kind of eating shop was copied by the hundreds across France and Europe. I wonder what Boulanger would think if he knew that the Thomas Lipton Soup Company recently tried to market a truly restorative soup: memory broth!

According to Judith Hooper in *All in the Mind*, Lipton Soups experimented with a chicken noodle soup laced with purified lecithin, a nutrient used to improve memories of people with Alzheimer's disease. It seems that lecithin contains raw materials the brain needs to make acetylcholine, a neurotransmitter. Alzheimer's victims have a deficiency of this chemical, causing them to suffer from memory loss.

Although Lipton's was not able to obtain the necessary government approval, the possibilities for its memory broth were exciting. They might have called it St. Anthony's Broth, after that patron of lost things, including lost memories. When you consider how difficult it is to remember all the data that's part of the contemporary information explosion—not to mention where you left your car keys—a memory broth could have become <u>the</u> *Soup de Jour*. I find that in the hurry of today's life, with so many things to remember, if I don't write something down, I forget it! Perhaps it's my age: as we grow older, our short-term memory decreases, but the good news about getting older is that our long-term memory increases!

In these days when *what is* looks like *all that there is,* with little hope of any real positive change, we need good long-term memories.

You would probably be startled if at Communion time, when handing you the chalice, the communion minister were to say, "Soup of Christ!" But that title may well be accurate—if we understand the meaning of the Soup Supper of the Eucharist. Hope does not live in fantasy but in memories. Since faith also is nourished by memories, Jesus instructed us to eat and drink at his table at the same time as telling us to "remember."

We are to remember how time and time again God has jumped into the lives of hopeless people and done something new. We need to be reminded about how God led the enslaved Jews out of Egypt, how God made spring come to the barren wombs of old Sarah and Elizabeth, and how God lit up Jesus' tomb—pitch-black in the despair of death—with the blinding light of the resurrection.

It seems that at times all of us suffer from some form of Alzheimer's. We forget, and so easily become hopeless. When you feel there's not much chance of anything being really different than it is at the moment, have yourself a bowl of soup. And as you sip it, take out the memories of how God has come to your rescue in past times. Remember too the old memories of our Jewish-Christian faith, and you'll be surprised at how hope will bloom again in the garden of your heart.

The Yo-Yo of Daily Prayer

The yo-yo has a long and interesting history. It appears in Greek paintings eight hundred years before the birth of Christ. Playing with the yo-yo was a favorite amusement of the nobility in the seventeenth and eighteenth centuries. We might even wonder if George Washington passed the time of day with his yo-yo as did the condemned French aristocrats who were awaiting their turn at the guillotine. In 1929 a toy maker named Louis Marx introduced the yo-yo to Main Street America, and it has remained a popular pastime of young and old.

Though we know the yo-yo as a toy, at first it was used as a stone weapon for hunting game. In the Filipino Tagalog language yo-yo means "come-come," and originally it referred to a lethal stone weapon, weighing four pounds, attached to a twenty-foot cord. Hunters would take this stone-thrower's boomerang, climb out on low overhanging branches of trees and wait for game to come near. Slinging the stone-spool attached to a long string allowed them to retrieve their weapon without having to climb down.

The yo-yo might also become a religious-educational toy. Play with a yo-yo at the end of your morning or evening prayer to see how your every thought, word or deed comes back to you, especially those used as weapons.

~ Chapter 5 ~

Ten Hummingbird, Pigeon and Hawk Feathers

Hire a Sin Eater

Some parish bulletins include want ads. If you needed some extra cash or simply wanted to be of assistance, would you answer this ad?

Wanted: A Sin-Eater at Tuesday night's funeral wake for Mrs. Geraldine Zelotes. Call 876-9021 or speak to the pastor.

Today, such a request might seem strange or puzzling, but several centuries ago it would have been a blessing for the poor of a parish. At one time it was a custom to hire poor people to come to wakes and take upon themselves the sins of the deceased. The hired "sin eater" would place a plate of salt on the chest of the dead person and on top of the salt a piece of bread. After praying an incantation, the sin eater would consume the bread—and with it the sins of the deceased!

It's hard to believe that someone could remove sins by a kind of holy osmosis, but it's even more difficult to conceive of anybody wanting to take on another's sins! I don't know about you, but my own sins are quite enough for me without adding someone else's. Granted, we believe the good news that Jesus was a sin eater, that he took upon himself our sins and the sins of the world. When he extends an invitation to "Come, follow me," however, we balk at becoming such sin eaters, twentieth century lambs of God.

Yet how much more beautiful and peaceful would be our world if we had a rash of that vocation. How harmoniously would our interactions flow if more people were willing and eager to take on other's faults, even those not technically sins. Every mistake awakens in us Adam and Eve's shame for their prehistoric failing, as well as their tendency to "pass the buck." Like them, when something goes wrong, we look for a sin eater, for some excuse that will lessen or deflect our responsibility.

If, like a feather on the Wind, you would like to share with Jesus the work of lightening the world's heavy burden of sin, look for occasions to take upon yourself others' errors and mistakes. When someone forgets to do something that you requested—and so is guilty of a "social" sin—you can become a sin eater. You might respond to another's failure with, "I'm sorry that I failed to make it clearer to you. I should have given you a note as a reminder." All of our lives abound with opportunities to lighten the pain when others make mistakes, even slight ones. And all your efforts to be a sin eater in your family and at work help prepare you for the heroic work of being truly Christlike.

Outside your home or workplace, the world's mistakes and sins await you as a co-lamb of God, a Christlike sin eater. Whenever you embrace a personal share of responsibility for the crimes of others, you acknowledge that you are a member of the Body of Christ. Such membership is proclaimed by more than Holy Communion. It is also made real by an un-holy communion, by a share in the sins of the Body.

In the olden days sin eaters came from among the very poor who needed the money and so were willing to absorb other's sins. That's fitting, because only "featherweights," the poor in spirit, should apply for the job. The paradox is that when we are in communion with Jesus' work of eating sin, we become infinitely rich. For, rather than feeding on sin, we are filled with the breath, the very life, of God.

Liturgical Dog Whippers

While recent years have seen a shortage of vocations to the priesthood and religious life, there has been no shortage of vocations to lay ministry. Perhaps you would like to be a lay minister but feel that all the jobs have been taken. If so, take heart because one branch of ministry may soon become available again. How would you like to apply for the position of liturgical dog whipper?

Until the end of the nineteenth century in England there existed just such a liturgical role for a lay person. Quite simply, it involved keeping order among the dogs in church! In those days pets, especially sheepdogs, accompanied their owners to church. The dog whipper's pastoral responsibility was to oversee the canine congregation, ejecting the badly behaved and excluding from entrance all troublesome hounds. Whips and dog tongs were the tools of this lay minister's trade.

Allow your imagination to play with the image of a congregation on Sunday morning that included barking and naughty dogs requiring a special usher. One might wonder why such a ministry as the dog whipper was necessary. Why, after all, didn't the dog owners themselves discipline their naughty dogs? Why couldn't the owners remove their barking or badly behaved dogs if they prevented some worshipers from praying? One also might think that if certain dogs didn't know how to behave in church and Sunday after Sunday caused trouble, their owners would stop bringing them. Then there would be no need to have a lay minister at the door to exclude them from entering.

Perhaps the sheepdog owners knew that their dogs didn't like going to Mass. Perhaps, too, the dogs were clever and took advantage of the knowledge that

their owners wouldn't discipline them the same way in church as they would at home. Another possibility is that the owners felt church was as good a place as any to teach them to heel and sit still. Or maybe owners welcomed church as a place where they could take a break from having to control their canines. In any case, the existence of the ministry of dog whipper seemed necessary.

If your imagination is still turned on, you can play with other possibilities. They could have had a doghouse in the back of church for the badly behaved pooches. It could have had a large window so that the owners could be with their pets and still see and hear the worship service.

If a "creation spirituality" becomes more popular and all of God's creatures are seen as having an integral part in the Great Feast, we may live to see a return to that tradition of dog owners bringing their pets to church. And it may just be that God not only loves the praise of all creation but also wants all creatures to worship together in their own way.

Still, human nature being what it is, some worshipers may still be distracted in prayer by barking dogs. And so, when the day comes that we all gather to worship under one roof, we may once again need the ministry of dog whipper. If you feel called to such a ministry, perhaps you should begin to prepare yourself for it today.

Stand Up and Be On Your Way

The next time you're confronted with whether or not to live the Gospel, don't sit down and think about it—instead, stand up! Standing for the reading of the Gospel at Mass is not only an ancient tradition, it's also a good idea if we want to do something with what we've heard. Standing instead of kneeling is an Easter statement, a sign that we have been raised up by the resurrection of Christ.

But now there is another reason for standing when faced with a difficult decision, a reason supplied by modern psychology. According to recent studies conducted at the University of Southern California, difficult decisions are made 20% faster when we're standing instead of sitting! Researchers believe the reason lies in the fact that the heart rate increases by about ten beats per minute when standing. This increase further stimulates the processes of the brain. So whenever you have to decide how to be faithful to the challenges of Christ, make that choice while standing.

Milo, the famous sixth century B.C. Greek wrestler, should have stood and thought before making what was to be the last major decision of his life. Milo was renowned for his physical strength and was a six-time champion at the ancient Olympic games. One day Milo came upon a tree in which woodsmen had left a wedge after unsuccessfully attempting to split the trunk. Milo sat down and eyed the tree for a short time before coming to the conclusion that with his great strength he could split the huge tree. When he hit the wedge with a mighty blow of his bare hands, the wedge sprang out, causing the split tree trunk to slam tightly on his hands. Trapped, Milo tragically became prey to vicious wolves, who tore him from limb to limb.

Jesus challenged us not to use physical might or authoritarian power when faced with a conflict, but rather to seek a solution through the power of love. Like poor Milo, when we find ourselves in a difficult situation, we are tempted to use whatever strength we possess. We exert authority, status or muscle instead of applying the way of the Gospel. While on the surface we might appear to triumph—since "might is right"—the success is often only skin-deep. The message of Easter is that the mighty exercise of power by the Roman Empire and the Temple leaders was only an illusion. Silencing Jesus by killing him proved to be a very short-lived victory.

Studies reveal that in disputes and arguments between parents and children, 90% of the time the parents are the winners! Naturally, the wisdom of age is superior to that of a child. But I wonder if the lopsided percentage is due to parental wisdom or more often to plain old parental power. To resolve any conflict of differing opinions in the way Jesus proposed takes time. A loving resolution requires time and effort to listen carefully to both sides and to respect the feelings of all involved. We therefore frequently choose the easier way to end an argument. Yet when arguments are resolved by force, are there ever any real winners?

The next time you are faced with a difficult decision or a conflict with someone, *stand up* and remember two things. First, recall as best you can how Jesus challenged us to resolve conflicts. Then, remember the story of the Olympic wrestler Milo.

Los Dos Carreteros

From the *Cuentos*, tales of the Hispanic Southwest, comes a story that should be heard by everyone who prays. "*Los Dos Carreteros*" is a tale about two men who had loaded their wagons with firewood on a hot summer day and were traveling along the *Villa Real de Santa Fe*. When they came to a steep hill, their wagons would go no further. It had rained earlier in the day, and that stretch of the road was still a quagmire. Try as they might, neither of the pair of oxen could pull their heavily loaded wagons up the slick hill.

One of the wagoners worked diligently with his oxen. He cracked his whip over their backs, cursing loudly to make them work harder. The other wagon driver didn't seem concerned about his problem. Lying down in the shade of a tree to take a nap, he said to himself, "God will get me out of this mess. I'll just say a few prayers before I take my nap. God will help me."

Now it so happened that the Lord and St. Peter were on their way to Santa Fe that day. They too were traveling the old *Camino Real* to see how their flock was living and to be of service to worthy people. When they came upon the two wagon drivers, the Lord said, "Come on, Peter, let's help this honest man push his wagon up the muddy hill."

So they both put their strong shoulders behind the wagon of the man who was laboring to get his oxen to pull harder. Soon the three had the wagon out of the mud and over the crest of the hill. The Lord and St. Peter then continued on their way to Santa Fe, paying no attention to the other man sleeping under the tree. As they walked, St. Peter turned and said, "Lord, I don't understand. Why did we help the man who was cursing his oxen but didn't

help the one who had remembered you in his prayers?"

"Well, Peter," said the Lord, "I can see that you still have some things to learn about human nature and about the ways of God. The man we helped did not curse from his heart. His anger came out of his intensity and his frustration, not from a lack of affection for his oxen. He is a good man who works hard and is concerned for the welfare of his family. The other man, however, is simply lazy! He thinks that I'll solve his problems if he only mumbles a few prayers before he goes to sleep. He is a hypocrite who remembers me only when he's in trouble. He can stay right where he is!"

This parable reveals how being a prayerful person isn't what it always appears to be on the surface. Trusting in God's providential care does not mean indifference to what happens. "Resigning oneself to the will of God" can often be used as an excuse for failing to plunge into life's problems deeply and with all one's energies. Really turning one's life over to God involves *caring passionately* as well as *not caring*.

Polish Boomerangs

The Poles invented the boomerang—no joke, I'm serious! Before the invention of the bow and arrow, somewhere around 22,000 B.C., the people of what is now Poland made boomerangs from the tusks of the great mammoths that roamed their land. It would take 13,000 years before that creative hunting weapon would reach Australia, the country with which we associate it today.

The purpose of this bit of trivia is not to present the Polish people as ingenious and creative—which they are, if you take into account all their gifts to culture in the areas of music, literature and science—rather, it is to awaken us. The boomerang traveled at a turtle's pace of 13,000 years across Eastern Europe and Asia before it arrived in Australia. Consider that American blue jeans, which became popular here in the 1960s, took only twenty years before they made the most wanted list in the Soviet Union and China.

What once took hundreds or even thousands of years to migrate across the world now takes only a few years or even days. To be alive today requires a virtue that all find difficult: the capacity to change. We no longer have the luxury of a slow evolutionary embracing of new inventions or ideas.

Those who resist change in their daily lives will experience a good deal of suffering and stress as the speed of progress and development continues to accelerate. If we wish to taste peace and happiness, we will have to learn the virtue of elasticity. A brief 2,000 years ago, Jesus proposed that virtue with his image of new wineskins. Be rigid, like old leather wineskins, and you will be burst open by the new wine of change.

If you find ideas like married clergy or women in the priesthood too novel, if you can't adjust to

changes in education, employment or things as simple as how young people dress today, here's a prayer that might help you acquire one of the most needed virtues for these turbulent times:

Come and awaken me, Spirit of the New,
    O God who makes all things supple and life-giving,
    and grace me with the gift of elasticity.
For high are the walls that guard the old,
    the tired and secure ways of yesterday
    that protect me from the dreaded plague,
    the feared heresy, of change.
Yet how can an everlastingly new covenant
    retain its freshness and vitality
    without injections of the new,
    the daring and the untried?
Come, O you who are ever new,
    wrap my heart in a new skin, ever flexible
    and ready to be reformed by your Spirit.
Come, O God of endless creativity,
    and teach me to dance with delight
    whenever you send a new melody my way.

Mohammed's Watermelon Wisdom

The followers of the Prophet Mohammed say that eating a watermelon produces a thousand good works! That's food for reflection, whether or not it's summer, when eating watermelons is one of the season's delights.

In parts of Africa and the Near East, watermelons form a regular part of the diet of many peoples. Among Egyptians, it is still a principal source of food and drink for several months of the year.

The above Islamic saying comes from a culture where watermelons are eaten mostly out-of-doors. In the process of eating one, the seeds drop to the ground and so are the source of countless other watermelon plants. But the expression contains more than just folklore for increasing the local crop of watermelons.

As disciples of Christ, our principal food and drink comes in the body and blood of Christ, Holy Communion. The Eucharist is our watermelon food not for a few months out of the year but every month and every week. While the wheat seeds have been ground into flour and the grape seeds removed from the wine, the Eucharist also has sacred seeds. It is these invisible seeds that we should drop along the roadside of our daily lives and so produce a thousand good works.

The next time you eat or even see a watermelon, be conscious of its seeds as more than something to spit out or push aside with your fork. Let eating a watermelon be a spiritual exercise in the meaning of the Holy Eucharist. While Communion incorporates us into the Risen Christ, that unity is also intended to last beyond Communion time. As we leave church, we should leave a trail of seeds of goodness that produces a great harvest of good works.

While scientists have given us seedless grapes and have even been able to create seedless watermelons, Jesus never intended to give us a seedless Eucharist. The question, however, is: Have we so cross-fertilized the Eucharist that it has become for us devoid of both the cross and its seeds?

We are told that Jesus went about doing good (See Acts 10: 38). If we are truly made one with Christ in the Eucharist, then we also should leave a trail of good works everywhere we go in life. The next time you come home from Mass, look behind you. As you go about your household duties or your work, see if you can tell whether you've just been to a great watermelon feast.

The Mystery of the Massive Chest

It's a quirk of our minds that we remember questions longer than we remember answers! Jesus must have been aware of that fact since his favorite form of teaching was to tell stories that conclude with the unasked question, "What does that story mean?" Parables are intended to prod us into proposing personal answers that will call forth changes in our behavior. Our own answers are intended to call us to conversion.

A good spiritual exercise would be to reread the parables of Jesus, trying to forget all the explanations that you have heard over the years. Instead of settling for old meanings, ask yourself what the parable means to you right now. As a way of awakening that attitude of questioning, here is a story that you probably have not heard before. When you've finished reading this ancient tale from the Near East, ask yourself, "What personal changes does this parable challenge me to make?"

There was once a wealthy middle-aged merchant who married a woman much younger than himself. One evening when he returned home earlier than usual, a faithful servant told him, "Your wife, our mistress, is acting suspiciously. She has a large wooden chest in her room, large enough to hold a man, yet she says it contains only family heirlooms. I believe there may be much more to it, but she will not allow me, your oldest and most trusted servant, to look inside."

The merchant went to his wife's room and found her sitting anxiously beside a massive wooden box. He asked her, "Will you show me what is in that chest?"

"Do you ask me that because of the suspicion of a servant or because you do not trust me?"

He answered, "Wouldn't it be easier just to open it up without questioning the possible motives?"

"I do not think so," she replied.

"Is it locked? If so, may I have the key?" asked the merchant.

His wife held up a large key saying, "I will give you the key, but first dismiss the servant." The servant was dismissed and the woman handed her husband the key to the box. Obviously distressed, she excused herself and left the room.

The merchant sat for a long time looking at the massive box and then called in four of his servants. Together they carried the unopened chest by the dark of night to a distant place on the grounds and buried it. The matter was never referred to again.

Thou Shalt Not Look for Loopholes

Recently I read a cartoon which delightfully captured how we often approach morality. The cartoon shows a monastery with an abbot standing at the door of a young monk's cell. "It has come to our attention, Brother Placid," says the abbot, "that you may not be happy with your vow of silence." Inside the cell a young monk is seated on his bed, and on his knee is a ventriloquist's dummy!

While I laughed at the young monk's clever way around his vow of silence, I also realized that the cartoon is a mirror. Its good humor reflects how we all try to bend laws to fit our needs by looking for loopholes. Medieval castles were constructed with narrow windows, often no more than slits in the walls, for archers to fire on attackers. These narrow windows were called "loops." By the seventeenth century, the term loophole was used for any clever way to escape a situation, especially a tricky way to slip out of observing some law.

Jesus was against loopholes. He taught his disciples, "Don't look for loopholes in the law. Rather, keep the spirit of the law" (see Mt. 5: 17-20). When Jesus came face to face with a law that he didn't feel applied to him he didn't look for a loophole. He simply went right through it! He refused to be saddled by social or religious laws he felt God also found unacceptable. Such rejection of law required courage since Jesus did more than "keep the law," he fulfilled it. To fulfill a law requires great love and also prayerful insight into the purpose of the law. It's much easier to look for a loophole or simply to break the law.

In recent surveys 84% of Americans said that they had broken the laws of their religion! That fact

could be seen as a sign of the decay of religious values and public morality, or it could be viewed as good news. It would be Gospel news if it meant that Christians were following Jesus by discriminating between God's laws and the legalities of religion. Over the centuries, Church scribes and lawyers, like the Jewish scribes of old, have become master loophole builders.

The next time you find yourself looking for a loophole in canon law, church law or even the Ten Commandments, consider instead a journey to the mountain of prayerful silence. On the high mountain-top in your heart, sit face to face with the Divine Lawmaker. Don't be in a hurry. Be patient and allow time for your heart to become accustomed to the brilliance of God's glory. Let that light gently fall upon all your motives, the reasons why you wish to not keep the law. Having finished that, ask God for the courage of heart not to break the law but to fulfill it.

Don't Let Technology Kill You

Labor day is our country's annual celebration in honor of the working man and woman. While the countless advances of technology over the past fifty years have eliminated or reduced many forms of hard manual labor, they have not reduced the number of hours we work! If anything, our vast army of mechanical servants seems to have reduced our leisure time. Perhaps one reason is that we make the same mistake as one of America's greatest ever manual laborers, the legendary black steel-driving champion, John Henry.

John Henry was a steel driver during the 1870-1873 construction of the Big Bend Tunnel of the Chesapeake & Ohio Railroad in West Virginia. Steel drivers used long-handled ten-pound hammers to pound steel drills into the mountain boulders, making holes for blasting explosives. In the midst of the construction of the Big Bend Tunnel a new machine was invented, the steam power drill. Similar to the appearance of robots on the assembly line, with their ability to outwork any human, the steam drill was proclaimed as more powerful than any man.

John Henry, who possessed a build like Arnold Schwarzenegger's, bet his foreman that he could outdrill any steam machine. Taking two twenty-pound hammers, one in each hand, he drilled two seven-foot holes in thirty-five minutes. The steam drill machine couldn't match that production, as it was able to bore only one nine-foot hole during the same time. John Henry had won the bet, but he lost his life! As a result of attempting to outwork the steam drill, he died when a blood vessel burst. Nevertheless, John Henry became a folk hero among gang laborers —and all hard workers. He symbolized the manual laborers' last stand against the machine age.

John Henry's early death in his contest against a machine holds a lesson for us in our get-ahead world. Don't try to compete with your computer, fax or any other modern machine. Remember the fate of poor John Henry when your machines tempt you to better them or even keep up with them. We can put ourselves in an early grave by forgetting that our machines are our servants, who can be, and should be, given the day off frequently (it's fine if they keep on working while we vacation). But the thrill of a challenge, the race to get more done before the day ends, can cause us to take on more than our human bodies can bear. Since technological labor-savers are relatively new, we have not yet learned how to consistently use them in a way that enhances our humanity.

If your daily work involves the use of a telephone, computer, typewriter or any technological marvel, try seeing it in a new way. As your workday begins, trace on it the sign of the cross. If you can, accompany that ritual sign with a mini-prayer such as, "Friend and co-worker, together with God, let us redeem the world." Practice thanking your machine when you turn it off at the end of the day. You may even want to give it a name, as were horses and beasts of burden who helped to lift the load of labor in the old days.

The work of *making holy* does not exclude machines. In "fax," that work of praying with our machines may be one of our greatest challenges as we travel the twenty-first century.

The Sound of Music

In Seoul, South Korea, there was a theater manager who thought *The Sound of Music* was too long a movie. He therefore decided he could reduce the running time of the film without doing damage to the plot by removing all the songs!

Singing and music aren't essential to either the assembly line or to public worship. The running time of the plot of your daily life, work and prayer also can be shortened considerably by removing all that unnecessary music. But is that really wise?

As the clock runs faster and faster each day, consider slowing it down with song. Sing to yourself as you pray, drive to work or clean the house. You may be surprised at how much enjoyment—and how much soul—will be added to your life.

~ Chapter 6 ~

Ten Feathers on
Love and Friendship

A Heart Transplant

Perhaps more than any other quality, love is what makes our hearts and spirits as light as a feather. Decorated with red hearts in all shapes and sizes, Valentine's Day is the feast of friendship and the holiday of lovers. It speaks of love notes and gifts of flowers or chocolates. But perhaps the best expression of love we could make is the gift of a heart transplant!

Would you be open to having a *misericordia* operation? It isn't the usual kind of heart transplant, since in Latin the word literally means "a heart of misery"! I'm sure many of you would say, "No thanks, I already have one!" The offer of a heart of misery may seem out of place when talking about affection, romance and the pleasures of love. However, while *misericordia* does translate as "misery," it also means "mercy."

Mercy—or compassion—is the quality that makes our hearts like that of the Divine Lover. When Christ gave us his one and only commandment, "to love," he didn't have Valentine's Day in mind. While the love of God is shown in affection and friendship, it is perhaps most vividly witnessed in the exercise of mercy. Rising above our own heart's salty sea of misery to show someone mercy is an ascension that requires the grace of God.

The paradox is that before we can show mercy, we must engage in mercy killing! To enter into the pain of another, I must first be dead to my own misery and need for mercy. Such a death does not deny personal misery, but attempts to transcend it in order to become a doorway to care for someone else who is suffering.

Compassion is not pity, feeling sorry for another's sad plight. Rather, as the name implies, it is a holy communion of passion. Compassion is a United

Suffering, which like the United States is a union of states and as such prefers the pronoun *us*. Compassion is a lover's virtue since it arises from a desire to share that which is most intimate. Mercy or compassion is possible only when we have felt the painful touches of misery's variety of sufferings, or at least when we have the ability to creatively imagine them.

Together with the courage not to deaden our own miseries, we need to move from self-concern (or self-pity) to other-concern. That sacred step is enabled by remembering the felt experience of present or past miseries. Such remembrance requires effort and grace since the human memory seems cleverly designed to erase painful memories and recall only pleasant ones. Prayer, however, allows us to override that design and be in touch with past miseries. When that happens, we are ready for a true heart transplant in which our old heart is exchanged for a Christlike heart.

Having truly felt the misery of shame when others laughed at you for making a mistake, in mercy you will never laugh at another's mistake. Having truly known the misery of being judged as inferior or being discriminated against for whatever reason, in mercy you will never discriminate against others. Having known the bitter taste of being left out or ignored, in mercy you will strive to include as many as possible in the circle of your love.

At the end of such a memory-prayer time, you will likely realize that a successful *misericordia* heart transplant has taken place. With your Christlike, miserable heart you and others can freely experience the merciful love of God.

A Holy Heart

You own a wondrous little pump the size of your fist whose work you probably take for granted. It weighs a little more than half a pound yet does enough work in twelve hours to lift a sixty-five ton tank-car one foot off the ground. Your heart pumps blood through about 100,000 miles of blood vessels, a distance equal to five round-trips between New York and Sydney, Australia.

This hardworking organ starts to form as soon as the embryo starts to develop. It begins as a simple tube that soon doubles back on itself. In the early stages of its development, the human heart resembles the hearts of various animals! In the first stage it is like the heart of a fish. The next stage, when the center wall is not fully developed, looks like a frog's heart. Then the heart resembles that of a snake, evolving later into a shape much like a bird's heart. At the final stage of development the human heart has right and left chambers that are separated by a wall. But is this the end of its evolution?

When Jesus told us to learn a lesson from his heart, he did not have in mind the knowledge you have just read. Jesus told us that his heart was *the* textbook. His heart, like ours, beat 4,200 times an hour as it pumped five quarts of blood through his body in about sixty seconds. What made his heart unique was that it was a fully evolved heart, a Sacred Heart. Jesus called his followers to take upon themselves the hard work of pushing their hearts to develop beyond their present stage. We all possess retarded hearts, since at some point our hearts have stopped growing before reaching the final stage of evolution.

St. Clement of Alexandria instructed us in how to continue that evolutionary work: "A real Christian

practices being God!" Now, being like God is a pretty tall order—it's hard enough just trying to be good. So St. Clement told us to *practice*.

When we practice something—whether it be a musical instrument, a sport or a trade—we repeat certain exercises over and over until they become second nature. And what should you practice if you want your heart to be fully developed? First, practice daily being unconditional in your love of others. Practice making your heart completely empty of all discrimination, bias and prejudice. Practice twice a day being good to both the just and the unjust, since Jesus said that God didn't let the gifts of sun or rain come only to those who merited them.

If you daily practice being like God in as many creative ways as possible, I promise you that your heart will continue to grow and mature regardless of your age. Moreover, as you practice, your heart will become so lightweight that the Wind will be able to carry it freely. And you will find that your evolved heart will be able to do even more wondrous things than it presently can as a simple human-animal heart.

Hooked on God's Love

Among the most pleasant of all leisure activities is one that Jesus gave to his followers as a special sacred vocation. He sent his disciples into the sea of humanity to be *fishers* for God. We usually think of that vocation as one restricted to religious professionals, but it's a vocation of everyone who is a disciple of Christ.

Actually, as the fourteenth century mystic Meister Eckhart tells us, it's God who is the Fisher and we who are the game. Love is the fishhook; but there's a problem. Anyone who has handled fishhooks knows they are very sharp and dangerous. So just as we stay clear of fishhooks, we tend to stay away from God's love.

We all know too well from the stories of the saints and from Scripture what happens to those who get hooked on God. Because we don't want our well-ordered lives upset, we avoid getting hooked on the radical love of such a demanding Lover who wants not just part of us but *all* of us! Now, a fisher can't catch a fish unless it takes the hook. So the hook must be hidden by some tempting bait, like a big, fat, juicy worm.

Jesus was the alluring bait that hid the hook of God's love. His humanity was the incarnation of God's love in the flesh, and, oh, how attractive it was! Sinners, those who were social and religious outcasts, all wanted to be near him. Why were persons who normally would have felt out-of-place in a religious environment so lured to someone who was so prayerful and religious?

Hidden in the answer to that question is the pattern for how you and I are to evangelize (to use a religious word), to go fishing in the sea of humanity. From all the Gospel stories it is clear that Jesus respected others, loved them for who they were at

the moment. He didn't preach at them, didn't demand their conversion as a requirement of his companionship. He was among them as one of them, loving them as God loves—unconditionally. Being hungry for such love, they swallowed him, hook, line and sinker. The paradox is that the more they were caught, the more they were liberated!

If we wish to go into the world as Christ sent us, as fishers, we need to make ourselves into the same kind of bait as was Jesus. Rather than attempting to make converts, let us simply love everyone we meet, the good and the bad, with unconditional love. If our love has strings attached to it, hidden motives other than loving as God loves, the "big" fish (who always get away) are clever enough to see the hook and will swim away.

Of course, the best way to go fishing in this Christlike way is to first be caught by the big, sharp hook of God's love and to wiggle with joy and delight. When we little fish are caught by unconditional love, we will become alluring bait for bigger fish. And again, fear not the hook, for to be caught by God is to be truly free.

A Love Stronger than Death

At the death of King George V of England in 1936, his son Prince David ascended to the throne as Edward VIII. In December of 1936, King Edward spoke to the British people over the radio. He told them that he could no longer carry out his duties as their king without the help and love of the woman he loved. That woman, however, was a twice-divorced American, Wallis Simpson. Such a "scandalous" marriage was out of the question for an English monarch. So great was the new king's love that after only ten months on the throne he abdicated his crown in order to marry Mrs. Simpson.

David and Wallie became the Duke and Duchess of Windsor and spent the rest of their lives as perpetual tourists. The former king was allowed to return to England only rarely during his lifetime. Though maintaining an aura of his royal birth, as exiles little remained for the couple but to grow old gracefully, which they did.

David Windsor died in 1972. For the next fourteen years his widow continued to put paper clips and fresh ink on his desk in his room. And over those many years, while she was still able, she would end each day by going to the study of the man who loved her enough to give up the throne of England. She would stand in the empty room and whisper, "Good night, David."

On Memorial Day it is our custom to visit and decorate the graves of those we have loved in life. It is a beautiful tradition of remembrance. But those beloved dead are not found in cemeteries! They live now in the mystery of God and are one in the Risen Christ. Jesus, before his death, promised his friends that he would be with them always, even to the end of the world. If Christ is with us and if the holy dead

are now in Christ, doesn't that mean they are also with us?

The touching evening ritual of Wallie Simpson reveals a belief that her David was not in heaven but was nearby. Life partners, parents or children who have died are as near as our belief system allows them to be. If we believe as Christ told us that the kingdom of God is with us, then are not the holy dead also with us?

A gossamer-thin wall separates us from the mysterious presence of God and those who are now one with the Divine Mystery. While death causes a real physical separation, we are called to live in the communion of saints, open to the nearness of those we have loved in life. That's not an easy awareness, but a tender love story like David Windsor and Wallie Simpson's can help us remember that, indeed, love is stronger than death.

A Romantic Revival

According to *Smith's Dieter's Guide*, a one-minute, extremely passionate kiss burns off twenty-six calories, which is about the same number of calories found in a small piece of chocolate. That's a valuable piece of information if you desire to live like a feather, if you are concerned about your weight—or your prayer. There's power in passion's heat to help you to be slim —and to be a saint.

Passion and prayer go together like spring and romance. Spring, like romance, frequently suffers temporary setbacks. Just when we think spring has arrived and are rejoicing in its warm weather, old winter can creep back with a chill. Many a love affair has also suddenly turned from the passionate delights of spring to the cold of late winter.

Jesus' whole life was a revival of romance. He echoed the command of Moses to return to God with passion, with all our hearts, and he showed us how to live with great passion. While being a Christian means living in that same pattern, when we pray or worship we're usually concerned about being reverential rather than being passionate. So often, too, we have a difficult time being fully present to our prayer, our minds being somewhere other than with our bodies. How often our prayer is like a typical conversation between spouses: "Excuse me, dear, what did you say? I was distracted for a moment."

Our personal relationship with God, like love for a partner, can easily cool from its original hot passion. With time it becomes a lukewarm, ho-hum duty. But just as spring follows drab, lifeless winter, there's hope for our prayer lives. As the intense heat of the sun warms the earth and calls forth fresh greenness everywhere, we can have a revival of our romance with God.

One way to begin is to pray less but with more passion and love. Among the old Jewish rabbis there was a saying that we should invest each word—each letter—of prayer with a passionate love for God. If you desire to infuse your prayer with a fullness of attention and love, try saying each word with as much love as possible. God doesn't care if you don't finish a psalm, a rosary or even a sentence of prayer, as long as you make each phrase of that prayer an act of loving with *all* your heart.

Whenever we passionately invest ourselves in something with either love or anger, our whole mind, body and heart are involved. At such times it is impossible to be absentminded toward what's at hand. The next time you find yourself distracted in the midst of prayer or worship, let it be a reminder to put more spring in your spirituality, to revive your romance with the Divine Lover.

Chosen as a Friend

Salman Rushdie, the author of one of the most controversial books of this decade, *The Satanic Verses*, recently said, "Books choose their authors; the act of creation is not entirely a rational and conscious one." The image of a poem, a recipe for a new dinner dish or some new invention roaming about looking for a home may strike you as a bit humorous. However, the notion that an idea can go around in search of someone to give it flesh is a novel and interesting one.

On second thought, Jesus wouldn't have found it a novel idea, for he said, "It is not you who have chosen me, but I who have chosen you" (Jn. 15: 16). How unheard-of! Unlike other spiritual masters whose disciples came to them requesting to be students, Jesus went in search of those who would become his followers. Those of us who are womb Christians, who were born into our religious faith and baptized as mere infants, might find equally mystifying the idea that Jesus chose us personally.

Before you dismiss the idea that you might have been specifically chosen by Jesus to be his disciple, ask yourself this question: "If that's really true, what are the consequences?" One result might be that you highly value and take great pride in your discipleship. How honored are those whom the great and famous —in any field—have chosen to be close associates. If our faith is not an accident of fate and we *have* been personally chosen, should we not be very proud of that fact? We might even become name-droppers, people whose pride in being a friend of someone famous is something to be proclaimed. Are you proud to be a Christian?

To be chosen by name to be a disciple is also to be selected as a personal friend. In calling us *friends* and not servants, Jesus invites us to step across the

threshold of his heart and share in his secrets. Those who are intimate friends of composers, writers and artists know all about the artistic projects they are creating. Likewise, Jesus shares with us his dream for a new world, a global and even cosmic creation. Pride should burst our buttons that not only do we have insight into the world's greatest vision, but we've even been invited to help create it!

Pride in that divine friendship gives birth to gratitude, which blooms forth in joyful prayer. For those who realize what it means to have been chosen, daily prayer ceases to be an obligation. For those who recognize the honor in being chosen, times of prayer are long-awaited opportunities for communion with their beloved friend. If your prayer times are not joyful reunions with an intimate friend, but only obligations that must be squeezed in, then maybe you should take some time to reflect on the real possibility that you *have* been chosen.

The Secret to Beautiful Eyes

Since the earliest times, women have yearned for beautiful eyes. Over the centuries cosmetic products such as mascara and eye shadow have been created to address that desire to heighten the beauty of the eyes. Originally, however, eye shadows were used not for beauty's sake but for protection from evil! Ancient Egyptians, both men and women, painted the area around their eyes to ward off the evil eye. They crushed the iridescent shells of beetles into a powder and mixed it with malachite to create the sacred green eye shade which was applied in a circle around the eyes.

Beautiful eyes, in both men and women, however, are less the result of external highlights than of internal luster. It is said that the eyes are the windows of the soul. They are also portholes of the heart. If your heart is full of love and peace, you cannot help but have beautiful eyes. If you look upon others, even strangers, with eyes of love, your eyes will radiate with beauty.

In the Hindu spiritual tradition it said that there are three ways of communicating spiritual awareness to others: through words, touch or a look. While the face can wear a mask to disguise the feelings of the heart, eyes cannot lie—nor can they hide the state of the soul. If you want irresistibly beautiful eyes, learn to put others first. Learn to think of their needs before yours and to look upon them with love regardless of their behavior, the kind of love that can reach their souls. While eye shadow is easier, it fails to create a penetrating beauty. Only a loving heart has that power.

Christian prayer is incarnational. It is more than words; it is prayer of the body. We are familiar with the "helping hand" as a form of prayer. Could we

not include the "loving eye" among our ways to pray? However, to pray with your eyes requires discipline and practice.

Under normal circumstances we look with our eyes as if they were camera lenses; our eyes simply mirror our inner feelings. Strong passions usually cause us to look with either love or hate upon others and upon life. While the eyes reflect our inner attitudes, the eyes can also become agents of change. A mother, for example, who looks with great love on her young child can literally melt the sadness, anger or pain the child is feeling. It's much more difficult, of course, when we do not feel loving at a given moment. But, again, making the eyes beautiful takes practice, especially when it's hard. If you're feeling upset with someone in your family, a friend, your boss or a sales clerk, try looking on that person with great affection and see what happens.

A mother has a special beauty in her eyes when she looks with care upon one of her children. Male or female, let each of us practice the prayer of looking upon others and the world with the eyes of a loving mother. Such a prayer discipline is truly a secret to having beautiful eyes, the eyes of Jesus. We are told that he "looked with love" upon the rich young man who wanted to follow him but was unable to give up his wealth (see Mk. 10: 17-22). He also looked with a mother's eyes upon Jerusalem, saying, "How often have I wanted to gather your children together as a mother bird collects her young under her wings" (Lk. 13:34). How long the world has yearned—and continues to yearn—for such beautiful eyes.

The Secret
of a Good Heart Attack

Among the ancient rituals of witchcraft in England was one formula that required inserting 385 pins into the heart of a horse, cow or pigeon! A variation of that rite dictated sticking the heart with nine new nails and nine new needles as well as countless pins; then the heart was set on fire. Magical rituals such as these were prescribed by the village witch whenever a disease struck someone's cattle, a lover was unfaithful or misfortune visited a village.

Paradoxically, if you felt you were being cursed, the cure for being thus bewitched was to stick a frog's heart full of thorns from a holy thornbush. Then the heart would be cooked in a pot of steaming water until done. Finally, it was buried in a grave seven inches deep and seven feet from the door of a church while repeating the Lord's Prayer backwards!

These black magic images of burning hearts stuck with nails call to mind the figure of the Sacred Heart of Jesus! The "white" or "good" magic of the heart of Jesus flows from his willingness to let his heart be pierced for our sins. The traditional picture of the Sacred Heart, familiar to all of us, shows a large heart encircled and pierced by thorns and engulfed in flames. That image speaks vividly about the fire of Jesus' great love, a fiery passion that would lead him to give his life for us and for the world.

Each time we look at a crucifix or an image of the Sacred Heart, a question should knock at the door of our hearts: "For whom or what am I willing to die?" It's hard enough to suffer pinpricks, yet Jesus proved his love by embracing death itself. If dying seems a bit radical as a proof of our love, we can ask, "How many nails and pins am I willing to have stuck

in my heart for what I love?" Before answering, imagine 385 tiny pinpricks or the pain of nine nails and nine needles being endured in the name of love. The Lover Jesus challenges us, "Come, follow me, and in the name of love let your heart become a pincushion."

Whenever we feel jabbed by unkind words or pricked by accusations or cruel jokes, we can embrace those heart attacks without having to strike back in anger or revenge. Feeling in our hearts the nails of injustice or the flames of hunger that consume the hearts of millions would be a similar kind of devotional prayer to the Sacred Heart of Jesus. While such living prayer seems painfully difficult, the paradox is that piercing the heart is *the* way to release joy from it. Only hearts willingly pierced in the pattern of the Sacred Heart are truly feather-light. Only such hearts allow love to ooze out, the kind of love that can change the world. And only such hearts made feather-light can be carried on the Wind back to God.

A Pet Parrot
Is Great for Self-Confidence

The renowned French impressionist painter Paul
Cezanne once acquired a bright green parrot. He
taught his pet to repeat one phrase over and over
again: "Cezanne is a great painter...Cezanne is a
great painter"!

As the classic cartoon character Pogo once said,
"We have met the enemy and he is us." Everyone
has a pet parrot. We have inner-parrots that repeat
again and again the voices we heard as children.
Let Cezanne be an example of how you should train
your parrot to only speak messages that affirm your
value.

Like Cezanne, select a single sentence today and
repeat it over and over to your pet parrot. Then,
like the famous pirate in *Treasure Island*, Long John
Silver, let your pet parrot ride on your shoulder
wherever you go—whether to work, play or prayer.

The Great Art Critic

Huang Erh-nan, a distinguished Chinese artist of the 1920s, is known for his ink masterpieces of butterflies and lotus flowers. His unique technique for creating beautiful works of art didn't even require a traditional brush. Huang would fill his mouth with black ink and then paint delicate strokes with his tongue!

You personally have at your disposal a similar "brush" with which to paint works of art—or make ugly graffiti. Fill your mouth each morning with love and your tongue will create beautiful works of art. Fill your mouth each morning with thanksgiving, and by day's end you will have made your world an art museum.

Perhaps at the final judgment, the only thing God will ask to see is your paintings!

~ Epilogue ~

The White Feather
of Maat

This final reflection is about the feather at the end of life. A single white ostrich feather was the symbol of Maat, the Egyptian goddess of justice. At their final judgment, Egyptian souls were led into the Judgment Hall of the Dead. There stood the goddess Maat holding the scales of justice and eternal life. In one pan of her scales Maat placed the heart of the deceased, and in the other pan she placed her white feather. If the dead person's heart was heavier than her feather, then he or she was forever banished from immortality. However, if the heart was made light as a feather by the kindness and love the person had shown in life, that fortunate soul was ushered into paradise. For all of us, possessing a heart able to float on the Wind like a feather is critical to eternal life. Blessed are the single-hearted, and the feather-hearted, for they shall see God.

As earthbound mortals, we live in a healthy tension with our small planet's laws of gravity. Without this magnetic force, simple daily actions like pouring a glass of water would be impossible. Yet within us is a primal passion to rise above that magnetic tug of gravity and to mystically fly. While life's burdens and problems can keep us grounded, we have the power to rise above them and be free as the wind. Ascending and being assumed upward are classic images for entering heaven at the end of life.

Wise are those who practice daily being light enough to float above the slings and arrows, the dead weights, of difficulties. Living like a feather on the Wind is made easier if at every time of prayer you can hear God whispering in your ear, "You are my beloved." That affirmation will free you of anxieties

about what to wear, or the source of your next meal, or your retirement. You are God's beloved! Let that be the central dogma of your personal creed and live in the providence of God's love and care for you.

As we learn from the legend of the Egyptian goddess Maat, the human heart also becomes light as a feather by each deed of love and kindness, every act of pardon and forgiveness. Letting go of trying to control others and the unexpected problems of existence can make you a featherweight. To lighten up is a critical spiritual principle that inspires us to laugh at ourselves and the gravity-bound desire to be taken seriously, to be considered as someone of importance. Cut yourself free from the deadweight of the need for respectability. Lighten up as you jettison clinging gray-haired grudges and sweep away the tired tracks of resentment trespassing in your heart. Cultivate a sense of humor which can unshackle your heart of the pride which is as heavy as iron. Play with your prayer and be cautious of solemn, serious worship of God which frowns on laughter and humor as disrespectful.

Don't hesitate to clown around in your quest for holiness. The great American circus clown Emmett Kelly created a character called Weary Willie. He was a sad-looking fellow, who never spoke or cracked a smile. His act was to juggle three balls while balancing a peacock feather on his nose. Yet when he dropped one of the balls and bent over to pick it up, the feather would never fall off his nose! Crowds roared with laughter as old Willie exposed himself as a phony—the feather having been stuck to his clown's red nose with putty. Churches are full of Weary Willies who never smile and live in fear that they will be seen for who they truly are. We all need to lighten up and let the feather float.

Practice wise medicine and try to have a good laugh at least three times a day. Be humorous with God and religion, for laughter is the best way to exorcise evil, which by its nature is as heavy as hell. Recall that by their sin Lucifer and the other rebellious angels fell like iron angels from heaven's heights into the depths of hell. So, a laugh a day can keep the devil away! Make mystical mirth an integral part of your spirituality as you laugh at yourself, at your follies and at life's plenitude of paradoxes.

To make yourself as lighthearted as a feather, maintain a whimsical attitude toward your spiritual path, be generous to a fault in loving and giving gifts, and let no heavy grudges climb aboard your heart as you daily live in a consciousness that you are floating on the Breath of God. I assure you, if you maintain these simple spiritual guidelines, when you stand before the judgment seat of heaven your heart will be as light as a feather.

A Feather in the Cap
of My Undertaker

I express my gratitude
to my undertaker,
Thomas Turkle,
and his associate undertaker,
Thomas Skorupa,
and their co-workers
at the Forest of Peace Undertakers
for their assistance.

Since 1698 *undertaker* has been used in America to mean a mortician, yet the word appeared three centuries earlier referring to anyone who undertakes a task. During that same period, *undertaker* was a customary term for a publisher.

Returning delightfully to its original meaning, I want to thank my undertaker, Tom Turkle, who undertook the enterprise of publishing a risky book such as this. I also appreciate the undertaking of the book's creative editor, Tom Skorupa, who artfully made dead letters look "so natural."

As its author, my hope is that this little *featherweight* book will be a feather in their caps.

Contents

Dedicated

to

Bishop Marion F. Forst

who for the past 18 years has
continuously confirmed me
and countless others

Other Books by the Author:
(available through the publisher or your favorite bookstore)

Prayers and Rituals

Prayers for a Planetary Pilgrim
Prayers for the Domestic Church
Prayers for the Servants of God

Contemporary Spirituality

The Lenten Labyrinth
Holy Fools & Mad Hatters
A Pilgrim's Almanac
Pray All Ways
Secular Sanctity
In Pursuit of the Great White Rabbit
The Ascent of the Mountain of God

Parables and Stories

The Quest for the Flaming Pearl
St. George and the Dragon
The Magic Lantern
The Ethiopian Tattoo Shop
Twelve and One-Half Keys
Sundancer
The Christmas Eve Storyteller

Feathers on the Wind

copyright © 1995, by Edward M. Hays

Library of Congress Cataloging-in-Publication Data

Hays, Edward M.
    Feathers on the wind : reflections for the lighthearted soul /
Edward Hays.
        p.   cm.
    ISBN 0-939516-30-6 (hardcover). — ISBN 0-939516-29-2 (pbk.)
    1. Meditations.   2. Christian life—Catholic authors.   I. Title.
BX2182.2.H377   1995
242—dc20   95-4948
                                                                            CIP

published by
Forest of Peace Publishing, Inc.
PO Box 269
Leavenworth, KS 66048-0269   USA
1-800-659-3227

printed by
Jostens, Inc.

1st printing: October 1995

Feathers

on the

Wind

Reflections for the
Lighthearted Soul

Edward Hays

FOREST OF PEACE
Publishing

Suppliers for the Spiritual Pilgrim